First published in Great Britain in 2020 by Wren & Rook

Text copyright © Matthew Syed, 2020
Illustration copyright © Toby Triumph, 2018 & 2020
Design copyright © Hodder & Stoughton Limited, 2020
All rights reserved.

The right of Matthew Syed and Toby Triumph to be identified as the author and illustrator
respectively of this Work has been asserted by them in accordance with the Copyright, Designs &
Patents Act 1988.

ISBN: 978 1 5263 6237 7
E-book ISBN: 978 1 5263 6238 4
Audio book ISBN: 978 1 5263 6239 1
10 9 8 7 6 5 4 3 2

Wren & Rook
An imprint of
Hachette Children's Group
Part of Hodder & Stoughton
Carmelite House
50 Victoria Embankment
London EC4Y 0DZ

An Hachette UK Company
www.hachette.co.uk
www.hachettechildrens.co.uk

Publishing Director: Debbie Foy
Managing Editor: Liza Miller
Consultants: Kathy Weeks and Dr Angharad Rudkin
Art Director: Laura Hambleton
Designed by Thy Bui

Printed in Italy by Graphicom

Additional images supplied by Shutterstock

# Matthew Syed

# Dare TO BE YOU

ILLUSTRATED BY

## Toby Triumph

wren
&rook

# CONTENTS

*Chapter 1* ................................... (06)

## DO YOU KNOW KID DOUBT?

*Chapter 2* ................................. (26)

## ONE SIZE ~~DOES~~ DOESN'T FIT ALL

*Chapter 3* ............................... (48)

## BEING DIFFERENT MAKES THE BIGGEST DIFFERENCE

*Chapter 4* ............................. (72)

## DON'T BE A CLONE

*Chapter 5* ............................. (88)

## GET CURIOUS

*Chapter 6* .......................... (108)

## BE YOUR OWN ACTION HERO

*Chapter 7* .......................... (126)

## COOL TO BE KIND

*Chapter 8* .......................... (150)

## BUMPS IN THE ROAD

*Chapter 9* .......................... (168)

## FOLLOW YOUR OWN PATH

INDEX .......................... (184)

REFERENCES .............. (188)

# 1

*I'm not sure if it was the smoke or the smell of burning that I noticed first. I am, however, totally sure of what I noticed second: the near collapse of Tim Preston. The colour draining from his face and his knees giving way under the weight of his growing panic. We both stared across the field, our eyes squinting against the flickering orange glow, our mouths wide open.*

## THE BAKERY WAS ON FIRE. ON FIRE. THERE WERE ACTUAL FLAMES.

*And billowing black smoke vomiting into the sky behind us.*

**Oh and, just by the way, it was our fault.**

It all started at the beginning of the school holidays after a reasonably bad end to the school year. My exams hadn't gone as well as I'd hoped and there had been an incident in a chemistry lesson involving potassium permanganate and Mr Long's trousers that I was really trying to forget about. So when my brother's friends Tim Preston and Philip Beck came over to our house, I decided that was my chance to put everything behind me and firmly establish myself as part of my brother's effortlessly popular friendship group.

Unfortunately it didn't work out like I'd hoped. They mainly just ignored me when I tried to join in – if I was going to get in with them, it was clear I was going to have to do something big. Something that would prove I was as cool as they were.

You see, Tim Preston was one seriously cool kid and Philip Beck was even cooler than that. They were the boys that everyone wanted to be friends with. Tim Preston seemed to be brilliant at **EVERYTHING**, and Philip was just so funny. And I wanted to be a part of that. So when they suggested we go over to the field and light a bonfire, I thought *This is my chance* and went to get the matches out of the kitchen drawer.

BONFIRE?
WHAT. ON.
EARTH.
WAS I
THINKING?

How was that **EVER** going to end well?

It wasn't. And it didn't.

The truth is, I wasn't thinking. I was mindlessly trying to impress Tim Preston, trying to make him and Philip Beck like me.

I had never lit a bonfire before in my life and I'm pretty sure they hadn't either. I'd only ever been to one bonfire before and that was a highly organised affair at the local community centre.

Just how bad an idea this was became clear when they suggested that I have the first go at lighting the fire. But I went along with it. We messed about with the matches for about twenty-three seconds – it wasn't all that interesting, especially not once I burned my thumb trying to prove that I was very experienced in the bonfire department. I repeat, in case you are in any doubt as to whether this was a bad idea – **IT WAS A TERRIBLE IDEA**.

We ditched the matches and ran further into the field. Tim and Philip started a wrestling game with me, which basically involved them throwing me to the floor repeatedly, and me pretending I thought it was hilarious when actually they were bruising my ribs.

We stupidly forgot all about the matches we had left by the back of the bakery.

That is, until we turned around and saw the flames.

9

# KID DOUBT AND THE CONSEQUENCES (NO, THAT ISN'T THE LATEST RAP COLLABORATION...)

We'll come back to that (major) incident shortly. Because it was in that moment – somewhere between being tackled to the ground by Tim Preston and Philip Beck and noticing that we'd set the bakery on fire – that I realised something. Something life-changing. Something that has stayed with me ever since.

Kid Doubt

So let's rewind a couple of years and introduce you to **Kid Doubt**. I first met him at school and he was quite distant at first. I didn't see him much, which was fine by me – he wasn't exactly a laugh a minute. But whenever he was around, I would start to feel uneasy. A bit anxious. A bit unsure of myself. Like I didn't fit in. And I didn't like it.

Around the time I first met **Kid Doubt**, I was reading *The Hobbit* by J.R.R. Tolkien. I can't tell you how much I was loving it. The story was so exciting, I just couldn't put it down. And so I took it with me to school. I usually played football at lunchtime, but that day I just wanted to read the next chapter, to find out about the next epic battle in this amazing fantasy world I was now a part of. I couldn't wait. So instead of heading straight out to the pitch, I went back into the classroom, got the book out of my bag and sat down to read.

Just at that moment, I felt an uneasy feeling and knew that **Kid Doubt** was around. Some of the other kids were staring at me through the window. They had the football in their hands and were pointing at my book and falling about laughing. I could see the shadow of **Kid Doubt** there too. He looked a bit like me but meaner, so I recognised him straight away.

All of a sudden I could feel my legs start to go wobbly and my hands getting sweaty. My mind started racing with thoughts like

**WHAT IF THEY DON'T LET ME PLAY FOOTBALL WITH THEM AGAIN? WHAT IF THEY CARRY ON LAUGHING AT ME? AND WHAT IF THEY DON'T LIKE ME ANY MORE?**

So I did something I regret to this day. (Not as much as the fire, but still quite a lot.) I pretended that I had been reading as a joke, to make them laugh. I tossed the book in the bin and ran out to join them on the pitch.

**Kid Doubt** didn't leave me alone for the rest of the day. He ran behind me on the pitch as we played and then sat behind me in class that afternoon. Watching me. Almost breathing on me. And when I walked home, feeling really disappointed that I had been so stupid as to throw my favourite-ever book in the bin, I'm sure I saw him smile. Like he was happy that I was uneasy.

# ;POILER ALERT)))

You have probably guessed this already, but **Kid Doubt** isn't actually a real person. In truth, he is just a feeling or a voice inside my head. You can't actually see him or touch him. But you can feel him and hear him, that's for sure. Sometimes the feeling can be a bit overwhelming. And I have found that thinking about him as a person has helped me to find ways to deal with him. So we'll carry on with that analogy if it's okay with you.

After that, **Kid Doubt** seemed to stick around. He wasn't always there but I learned that he could turn up anywhere and at any time. He was always miserable, always hunched over, his grey face arranged in a permanent frown.

And I started to worry. About all kinds of stuff that had never really worried me before. I started to think that my friends didn't like me, that maybe I wasn't cool enough, that my clothes weren't good enough, that even just being me wasn't good enough.

I started to behave differently when **Kid Doubt** was around too. I'd see him smirking if I got anxious, so I'd get all loud and start acting the fool in class so that everyone would laugh. I thought that if I could

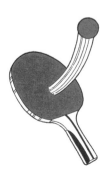 make everyone laugh, then maybe they'd like me more. And I started skipping table-tennis practice.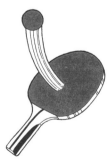

*Oh, did I mention that I am quite good at table tennis? Really? I haven't managed to get that in yet?! That I am absolutely mega at ping pong?* **WEIRD.** *My brother says I can't stop going on about it, but I knew he was wrong. We're a whole 1,250 words into this book and I haven't even mentioned anything about it. (Not even the two Olympics I went to. Yep.* **TWO.**)

Under the influence of **Kid Doubt**, I had started to skip practice. I didn't want to, I loved it. But every time I saw **Kid Doubt** near the training hall, I'd start thinking about that incident with *The Hobbit* and the football. I'd get so anxious about everyone laughing at me that I decided I'd rather not go.

**Kid Doubt** being around was really starting to hold me back. And it wasn't something I had planned for. I didn't know how to handle it. But he was making me anxious. He was making me do stupid things. And worst of all, he was making me want to be someone else – anyone else – but me.

And that is how, in probably the worst incident of my life to date, I ended up almost burning the bakery down.

**Kid Doubt** was definitely in the mix that day, laughing at me when my brother and his friends weren't interested in my attempts to be part of the crew. Making me anxious that I wasn't cool enough to fit in. Encouraging me to do things that I knew were a really bad idea.

13

After Tim Preston and Philip Beck recovered from their panic at seeing the flames, they were off. Tim's parting words were something like:

**THIS IS NOTHING TO DO WITH ME, YOU IDIOT.**

And so there I was – well, there **WE** were. Me and **Kid Doubt**. And about eight firefighters. People from the local streets started to arrive to look at the damage.

And then I saw my mum driving towards the scene. There was no doubt it was her. I could spot her a mile off because the words **SYED BROTHERS** were emblazoned in enormous, bright orange letters on the side of the car. (Yes, you read that right! There's more to come on this later ...)

## MY HEART SANK.

Never mind the potassium permanganate and the trousers. Things were about to go from bad to whatever is much, much worse than staining your chemistry teacher's best outfit pink.

# THE CONSEQUENCES...

Thankfully no one was hurt in the bakery fire. In fact, not even a croissant was actually burned in the end. It was Sunday and the bakery had been shut. But we were extremely lucky that it wasn't more serious. And I really did pay, I was grounded for a **VERY LONG TIME**. That summer, I was only allowed out of the house to scrub the soot off the bakery's brickwork, which took six whole days, or to wash the car (the one with **SYED BROTHERS** on the side).

But, in the end, I owe a lot to that incident. And I don't just mean the obsessive fear of matches that I still have. No, on my sixth day of scrubbing those bakery walls, I had an epiphany.

I realised that the fire had happened because for too long I had let something else, *someone else* – **Kid Doubt** – guide the things I felt and did. I had almost burned the bakery to a cinder in the pursuit of making Tim Preston like me. I'd even given up reading *The Hobbit*.

And suddenly I knew that I didn't need **Kid Doubt**. In fact, things would be a whole lot better if I believed in myself and did the things I actually wanted to do. After all, **Kid Doubt** is no friend. What kind of a friend wants you to feel rubbish? Wants to make you act differently just to fit in? Wants to make you anxious and nervous? That is no friend **AT ALL**. That person is just going to hold you back.

And so I made a pact with myself: I decided I wasn't going to let **Kid Doubt** make me anxious any longer. I was going to follow my **OWN** path, not someone else's. I'd finally figured out that **THAT** is what being cool *really* looks like. From then on, I promised myself that I was going to:

 **1** MAKE FRIENDS WITH PEOPLE WHO LIKED ME FOR *ME.*

 **2** MAKE CHOICES THAT I FELT WERE RIGHT FOR ME.

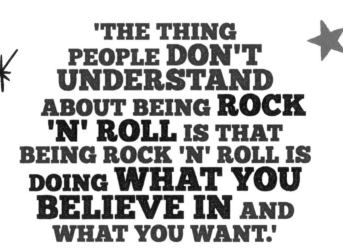

'THE THING PEOPLE DON'T UNDERSTAND ABOUT BEING ROCK 'N' ROLL IS THAT BEING ROCK 'N' ROLL IS DOING WHAT YOU BELIEVE IN AND WHAT YOU WANT.'

CHRIS MARTIN, LEAD SINGER OF COLDPLAY

One thing I learned quite quickly after making my pact is that **Kid Doubt** is quite the 'hanger-on'. I had vowed to ignore that grey and miserable face if I ever saw him again. But of course, I did see him again. Often. You name it, if there is a party, an exam, a competition, a play rehearsal or a school trip, he'll be there, trying to get an invite.

So it wasn't long before I started to wonder why **Kid Doubt** had such an effect on me. Why did I want everyone to like me so much? And how was I going to overcome the anxiety that **Kid Doubt** made me feel when I could see him smirking at me? I needed to develop strategies to help build my confidence. To figure out how to refill my tank of resilience when **Kid Doubt** left it empty.

As I got a bit older, I turned these strategies into a kind of plan. A manifesto for daring to be **ME**. And if I was feeling unsure, I would run down the items in **The Plan** to give myself the confidence to follow my own path. The confidence to question the world around me. And the confidence to make changes if things weren't working as well as they should.

# THE PLAN

## (A MANIFESTO FOR DARING TO BE YOU)

**1** **Make friends with people who like you for YOU.**
If you haven't already found them, keep looking.
They are out there, I promise.

**2** **Make choices based on what you feel is right.**
**For YOU.** Don't listen to whatever **Kid Doubt** is suggesting.

**3** **Don't blindly copy other people. Be YOU.**
We'll get to this later. There's a bit of science to this.

**4** **Ask questions. Keep asking questions. Make things**
**work for YOU.** Don't take the current situation at face value.
Get curious about why things are the way they are – and see if you
can make them work better for you.

**5** **Don't be afraid to do things at YOUR own pace.**
Be brave enough to ask for help and slow down if you need to.

### **6** **YOU** should be prepared to be flexible.

You might not find your own path straight away. You might need to change it up a few times before you find what really works for you.

### **7** Be kind. And don't listen to anyone who isn't kind towards **YOU**.

Don't throw up over this one. It sounds a bit sickly, but I am going to show you that being kind works in your favour. And besides, who wants to start acting like someone else's **Kid Doubt**?

### **8** Make it happen. Don't wait. Get out there. It is down to **YOU**.

**Dare to be different. DARE TO BE YOU!**

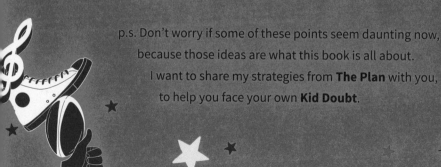

p.s. Don't worry if some of these points seem daunting now, because those ideas are what this book is all about. I want to share my strategies from **The Plan** with you, to help you face your own **Kid Doubt**.

# TRACK DOWN YOUR KID DOUBT

Everyone has a **Kid Doubt**. And I mean **EVERYONE**. Even if they tell you otherwise. Even if they appear to be brilliant at everything. Even if they appear to have so many friends they could fill Wembley Stadium. Even if they appear not to have a care in the world. Because

# (((SPOILER ALERT)))

**Kid Doubt** has about 7,700,000,000 brothers and sisters. (Imagine the family reunion!) Every single person on the planet has their very own **Kid Doubt**. Even really famous and successful people.

## 'I HAD TO OVERCOME THE QUESTION "AM I GOOD ENOUGH?"'

MICHELLE OBAMA, FORMER FIRST LADY OF THE
UNITED STATES AND KICK-ASS CAMPAIGNER,
ON HER KID DOUBT

# 'ANY MOMENT, SOMEONE'S GOING TO FIND OUT I'M A TOTAL FRAUD, AND THAT I DON'T DESERVE ANY OF WHAT I'VE ACHIEVED. I CAN'T POSSIBLY LIVE UP TO WHAT EVERYONE THINKS I AM AND WHAT EVERYONE'S EXPECTATIONS OF ME ARE.'

EMMA WATSON, AWESOME ACTRESS, CAMPAIGNER, FORMER GRYFFINDOR AND OCCASIONAL SELF-DOUBTER

Your **Kid Doubt** might look different to mine. They might be bigger, smaller or even less funny (although that would be hard to imagine). They may not be a 'he'. But all the **Kid Doubts** have one thing in common – they are all trying to hold us back. To make us feel that we are not perfect, that we should try and be like other people, that we shouldn't enjoy the things we do – and should enjoy things we don't. Making us feel anxious about the goals we hope for, and nervous about our choices.

We need to look **Kid Doubt** in the eye and start getting happy with being exactly who we want to be. Why? Because we are Awesome. Why else? Because sometimes we don't *feel* Awesome. Honestly, it is exhausting worrying, trying to fit in, trying to be somebody else. Not to mention time-consuming. One piece of research by 72 Point suggests that people spend nearly two hours worrying **EVERY SINGLE DAY**. That's nearly twenty-eight days a year! The whole of February, twenty-four hours a day.

**NON. STOP. WORRYING. UGH.**

So, if we could find a way to boost our confidence and be happy being who we want to be, there would probably be a whole lot less to worry about. And then we'd have a whole lot more time to do the things we really enjoy (like, for me, table tennis. Did I mention…? Oh okay, yes, I did).

And that is what **THIS BOOK** is for. I am going to prove (a big claim, you can vote me off the show if I don't) why you should dare to be yourself. That's right, this is a book about you (well, actually, it is quite a lot about me). But seriously, this book really is about **YOU**. About the person you are now, the person you were ten minutes ago as well as two years ago. About the person you will be tomorrow and the day after that, the year after that and into the future. **YOUR** future. Like it or not, you are you. So let's decide, right here, right now, to make sure you **LIKE** yourself.

I'm going to bust the idea that anyone is 'normal' – which means there is no point in aspiring to fit right in and be, well, 'normal'. I am going to show you that copying other people can be a real waste of energy sometimes. I'm going to show you that there isn't just one path to success. There are loads of different paths and what works for you might be totally different to what works for your best friend or your older sister. I'm going to show you that the best ideas come from people who think differently to the crowd, so stick with your own thoughts and be confident enough to find your voice. I'm going to show you that you should **DARE TO BE YOU**. Because **THAT** is your pathway to confidence and happiness.

Now, let's get on with it while **Kid Doubt** isn't looking. And we'd better be quick. Because he's sure to be back. And we need to be ready ...

# OVER TO YOU

## MEET YOUR KID DOUBT

Do you have a **Kid Doubt** that holds you back sometimes?
What are some of the things that you worry about?

O  Take a blank sheet of paper. If you'd like to, you can draw
   your **Kid Doubt** on one side of the sheet and yourself on
   the other side.

O  Underneath **Kid Doubt**, draw some thought bubbles.
   In each one, write down something that you feel unsure,
   nervous or worried about at the moment.

O  Now imagine how you would like to be feeling instead,
   if **Kid Doubt** was nowhere to be seen. What are the
   things you might need to think or say to **Kid Doubt**
   to make that happen?

ONE SIZE ~~DOES~~ DOESN'T FIT ALL

# 2

*Normal.* *It sounds like quite a safe place to be, doesn't it?*
*But what does it mean?*

*Quite like most other people? Part of the crowd?*

Very little for **Kid Doubt** to be laughing at there, right? Perhaps that's
why so many of us spend so much time trying to be as similar to those
around us as we possibly can. But it can mean we end up doing things we
don't like, don't enjoy or don't even believe in just so that we fit in. I once
pretended to be in to skateboarding. I wasn't. I never even tried it. I didn't
want to break my leg, which I needed quite a lot for being good at table
tennis. But everyone else seemed to be talking about ollies and getting
'air'. I didn't want to look like the fool who thought that a kingpin was
something Prince Charles might use to hold his trousers up.

What did I do? You'll never guess, so I'll tell you. I carried a
skateboard to and from school. Every day, for a whole year. Just so
the other kids thought that I was like them. Normal. On The Regs.
Ordinary, typical, average.

Now, I think we need to take a step back here. It's worth thinking about where this idea of a 'normal' person came from in the first place. What **IS** normal, anyway? And why do so many people seem to want to be it?

Let's start with an example. The picture below shows two people. Both are thirteen years old and in the same class at school. It's me and my best friend Mark (kind of).

Me

*I am not sure if the art budget ran out but I was asked to draw this picture myself. Our illustrator, Toby Triumph, clearly has nothing to worry about.*

Mark

We were both pretty 'normal'. We thought so, anyway. We liked the same stuff, laughed at the same jokes, lived in similar houses. All pretty average, really – **AND** we were both a bit strapped in the pocket-money department.

So we came up with a fantastic idea. We decided to share our clothes. Yes, you read that right.

This seemed like a totally amazing plan. We were both about the same size (or so we thought). And we both really wanted an Adidas Firebird tracksuit. I love a tracksuit, and this one (to us, at least) was the very **DEFINITION** of what it meant to have style. But our parents had told us both that we'd need to save our pocket money if we wanted 'fancy' clothes. So we did. And that is when we thought of ...

The
BRILLIANT
SCHEME

If we pooled our cash and bought just **ONE** Firebird tracksuit and shared it, we'd only need half the money and we could save it twice as fast!

We had it all worked out. Mark was going to wear it on Saturday (while I wore my table-tennis kit) and I could have it on Sunday (while he wore his best shirt to church). Perfect. And after a brief argument over the details (he wanted blue, but I thought black was more my colour), we bought it. We thought we had really surpassed ourselves with this one.

**Except we hadn't.**

Because although we were both average-sized teenagers, it turned out that we weren't very similar. At all.

We bought the Firebird in a medium size. We were both a medium size in the shops.

But as you can see from my brilliantly drawn stick men, Mark's legs were a bit shorter than mine. So he had to have huge turn-ups on the bottoms. They didn't look as good as we had hoped. And because my legs were a bit longer, you could see a lot of my ankles. That looked even worse.

My waist was a bit smaller than his too. So I had to get some extra elastic sewn into the waistband to keep them up when it was my turn to wear them. That was an expense we hadn't planned for.

So far this scheme wasn't going quite as well as we had thought it would.

The Firebird top was an even bigger problem. Mark's chest was bigger than mine and he couldn't quite do the zip all the way up. It looked like he had bought a skintight version and I was convinced he was stretching it. And my torso was a bit longer than his, so the top wasn't long enough to meet the bottoms. It felt like I was wearing the crop-top edition.

## IT WAS A FASHION DISASTER.

In trying to buy an outfit that would fit both of us, we had ended up with an outfit that didn't fit **EITHER** of us!

Although at first glance we looked pretty similar, we were different in almost every way. Our heads, arms, legs and waists were actually not that similar at all.

° ° ° ° ° ° ° ° ° ° ° ° ° ° ° ° ° ° ° ° ° ° ° ° ° ° ° ° ° ° °

*(And that's just our bodies. Don't even get us started on what music we each liked or our favourite flavours of crisps. Salt and vinegar is mine, in case you're wondering. Mark's was prawn cocktail. We really were **VERY** different.)*

° ° ° ° ° ° ° ° ° ° ° ° ° ° ° ° ° ° ° ° ° ° ° ° ° ° ° ° ° ° °

So trying to find **'ONE SIZE FITS BOTH OF US'** just didn't work. What we really needed was something that worked for each of us.

So the takeaway here is …

**ONE SIZE DOESN'T FIT EVERYONE AT ALL**

Now, this kind of problem wasn't unique to us living in Reading in the eighties. The world is, shockingly, still filled with plans and sizes and solutions that are supposed to work well for most 'normal' people. But just like the Adidas Firebird, they actually end up working for almost no one.

Let's have a look at some other examples.

# PILOT PALAVER

Just think about this. In 1926, the US military decided to use the idea of One Size Fits All to design the perfect cockpit for their fighter planes.

The air force collected measurements on hundreds of their male pilots (back then, no one thought that girls could be pilots, so they weren't included. Fools). They calculated 'normal' height, 'normal' arm length, 'normal' leg length, 'normal' reach and other useful metrics. Using this data, they created the 'perfect' cockpit with seats and helmets, buttons and steering columns, pedals and levers, all perfectly sized for the perfectly sized pilot.

**BRILLIANT, THEY THOUGHT.**

Except it really wasn't. You're probably already there with this one. It was me, Mark and the Firebird tracksuit all over again. But the US military took a bit longer to work it out.

Twenty-five years after these cockpits were designed, the air force was perplexed about why their pilots kept crashing. Apparently seventeen pilots crashed in a single day once. After a while, they began to think it might be the design of the cockpits that was to blame.

A guy called Gilbert S Daniels was working for the US military and decided to look in to this. He took ten of the most relevant measurements (like height, arm length, chest width, reach and so on) from just over 4,000 currently enlisted pilots. From this, he calculated the ten dimensions of the so-called 'average' pilot. The perfect arm length, the normal reach, the standard height, that kind of thing. So far, so repetitive.

But then Gilbert went one step further. He decided to see how many of his 4,000 pilots were **ACTUALLY** 'normal'. The air force expected loads of them to be 'normal'. Why wouldn't they be? After all, they hired excellent pilots and they had designed a perfect cockpit for them to fly in!

Guess how many of the 4,000 pilots were 'normal'? Guess how many of the 4,000 pilots had the arm length and chest size and other measurements that the cockpit was designed for?

Go on, have a guess?

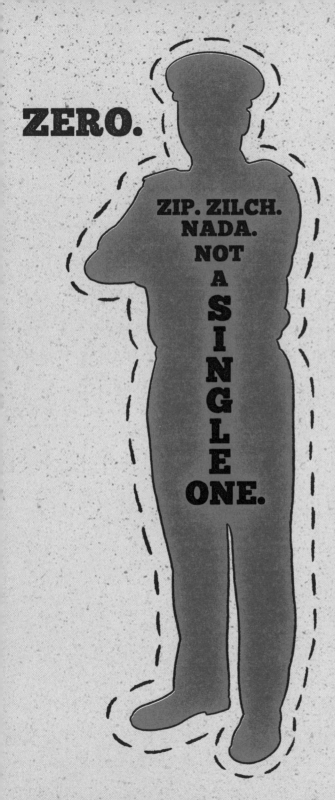

# ZERO.

**ZIP. ZILCH. NADA. NOT A SINGLE ONE.**

None of them had the ten measurements the cockpit had been designed for.

None of the pilots were **'NORMAL'.**

They had designed a cockpit that worked for precisely... **NO ONE!**

And that is why they kept crashing.

Read on for another example...

# YOU ARE WHAT YOU EAT?

For many years we have been told all kinds of conflicting advice about what is good for us to eat. Phrases like 'a balanced diet' or 'five portions of fruit and veg a day' or 'low fat' are flying around all over the place. It can be difficult to keep up. And when we talk about what is good for 'us', we mean basically the whole human race. So, a pretty large group.

In fact, most dietary advice is based on what is thought to be good for a 'normal' person. A single person who we are all supposed to be like.

**BUT.**

Did you know that in our intestines we each have tens of trillions of micro-organisms? Seriously! We have a whole army of bacteria in our guts helping us to digest our food. It's a complicated business you see, digestion. Getting the nutritious stuff out of the food and into our bodies, leaving the bad stuff behind, killing any really toxic stuff. It takes trillions of these little guys to do it properly (1,000,000,000,000 – that's how many zeros a trillion has). There is a whole ecosystem going on underneath the belly button.

I know, it's mind-blowing. Or **GUT-BUSTING** at the very least.

But here is the important thing. We each have a
**TOTALLY DIFFERENT** combination of organisms. We
have some in common, but the rest (maybe about 20 trillion
– as you can imagine, they are quite hard to count) are a combination
that is **UNIQUE** to each person. No one else has them. It's a kind of
(quite slimy) intestinal identity card.

This makes quite a big difference, as it turns out. Since we are all
unique, it seems sensible that we might each digest different foods in
different ways. So basing our eating habits on what might work for a
'normal' person just doesn't make sense. We are different in literally
trillions of (bacterial) ways from that 'normal' person!

Soon we will have the technology to work out exactly what diet
is right for **YOU**. Whether **YOUR** trillions of organisms might
digest carrots better than broccoli. Or tuna
better than bacon. You'll be able to tell
whether **YOUR** organisms don't like
milk so that when you are served it
at school or on your cereal, you'll
be able to say no.

No more 'one plan for everyone'
that probably doesn't work for anyone
at all.

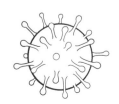

*WARNING: Don't use this as an excuse to assume you are the one person on the planet who should live on a diet of ice cream and pick 'n' mix. You probably aren't that person. I'm sorry to say it isn't likely that **ANYBODY** is that person.*

# IT MAKES YOU THINK, DOESN'T IT?

For centuries we have had plans and advice geared to the idea of a 'normal' person. And those plans might not work for us as individuals **AT ALL**.

# THE HISTORY OF 'NORMAL'

Where did the idea of being 'normal' actually come from anyway? Because it hasn't been around since the dawn of time.

In fact, 'normal' is something we invented, and relatively recently too.

A scientist called Quetelet (think 'Kettle Lay' in case you need to say it out loud) was working as an astronomer in Belgium in the 1800s. But there was a revolution going on at the time, so he had to pause his astronomy and instead got interested in the census that Belgium was conducting.

Officials were collecting information about all kinds of things for the census. Like how many people were born or were dying each year. And how many people were getting married. Quetelet realised that this type of data collection was happening all over the place, and that he could find information about what diseases people were catching, how tall they were, what jobs they did and even what stuff they bought.

Quetelet collected a lot of information both from the Belgian census and from other countries that were collecting data too. He started calculating things like the average size of a Scottish man's chest (clearly essential info in the nineteenth century). And then moved on to other things like average weight (not just of Scottish people this time), average height and the average age people got married. A whole range of averages.

Quetelet was one of the first people to try to use maths and averages as a way to define what 'normal' looked like for a group of people. It wasn't a totally terrible idea. He thought that a 'one size fits all' approach might make things easier. And sometimes it does. But it also means that nothing is quite right for us as individuals either. Think Firebird tracksuit.

But there was **ANOTHER PROBLEM**. An even bigger problem. And that was the way in which Quetelet started to think of his 'normal' person.

You see, he started to almost worship this 'normal' person he had come up with. Quetelet fell in **LOVE**. With being normal.

He believed he had discovered the perfect person. The person who was of normal height and normal weight and got married at the normal age and had the normal number of children. He thought of this normal person as the closest thing to **PERFECTION** anyone might hope to be.

**CAN YOU SEE THE PROBLEM NOW?**

Quetelet thought that anyone who differed slightly from the 'normal' he had calculated was an error. Was not perfect. Had **ACTUAL** in-built mistakes.

He had invented the idea that if we are not 'normal', we are not good enough. Not perfect.

AND EVER SINCE, WE HAVE BEEN **WORRIED** ABOUT NOT BEING **PERFECT**, OR **NORMAL**. INSTEAD WE WANT TO BE **AVERAGE**, OR JUST LIKE **EVERYONE ELSE**.

It is a massive problem, and one we kind of invented for ourselves. Because, as I hope is now clear, no one is really Quetelet's definition of 'normal'.

'IF YOU
ARE ALWAYS
TRYING TO BE
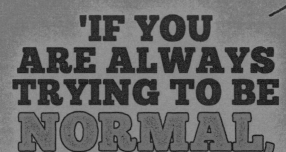
NORMAL,
YOU WILL NEVER
KNOW HOW
AMAZING
YOU ARE.'

MAYA ANGELOU, INCREDIBLE AUTHOR

# SO WHAT NOW FOR OUR 'NOT SO NORMAL' FUTURE?

The good news is that we are slowly but surely ditching our 'one size fits all' approach. We are embracing our uniqueness. In the future we are hopefully going to worry a lot less about trying to fit in with everyone else.

There are great examples of this happening already...

 ## LEARNING YOUR WAY

Hooray! Finally! I'm not sure why it took us so long to figure this one out, but we are at last realising that while everyone is capable of learning, we all have different **WAYS** of learning. Research carried out by Benjamin Bloom at Chicago University in the 1950s and 60s as well as by the Bill and Melinda Gates Foundation more recently has shown that students learn better when they are able to go at their own pace. So what suits you best might be totally different to what suits the person next to you in class. Whether you are a visual learner, whether you have dyslexia, dyspraxia or autism, whether you learn best in the morning or whether you might just need a little more time, there is a method that will be right for **YOU**. You just need to find it and work on it.

The brilliant news is that schools are getting much better at figuring out ways to help individuals learn in the best way for them.

OUR

## ⭐ MEDICINE JUST FOR YOU

The pills we take when we are unwell are becoming personalised too. Unsurprisingly (again, why did it take us so long to figure this out?), medicine is much more effective when it is designed for you and your exact body. It is a seriously complicated piece of kit – everyone has different hormones, fat levels, blood cells and so on. So it makes total sense that a drug that works best for your combo of cells might not work quite so well for your best friend who has a different combo.

## ⭐ MUSIC GOES PERSONAL

In days gone by you'd have to listen to things called tapes or CDs (ask your dad). These chunky things were expensive and took up space. So you'd save your money, choose your favourite bands, spend your savings on perhaps two albums and then listen to them on loop. It meant that if you liked Ed Sheeran and Taylor Swift and wanted to listen to 'Shape of You' and 'Shake It Off', you'd also have to hear a lot of album tracks that you didn't necessarily like as much. You also probably didn't hear much of anything else

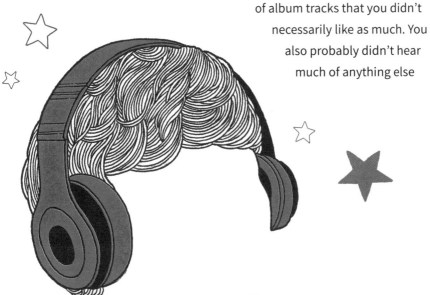

44

(unless your parents had an old Wham! album, and then you might get a bit of 'Club Tropicana' thrown in once in a while). Not any more. Now, music streaming services allow you to listen to any track you like at any time. You can build a personal playlist full of **YOUR** favourite songs by different artists. It's cheaper and you don't need a massive shelf in your spare bedroom to keep all the tapes. These streaming services will even suggest songs by new bands that **YOU** specifically might like based on things **YOU'VE** listened to before.

Hopefully, you see the theme here.

# THE FUTURE IS GOING TO BE ALL ABOUT YOU.

What **YOU** like, what **YOU** need and what makes **YOU** happiest.

Because you are the same as precisely…no one. Which means that the idea of wanting to 'fit in' or be 'just like everyone else' is **POINTLESS**.

After all this, you'll be glad to know that I eventually decided to …

And Mark and I gave away the Firebird tracksuit. (To my brother – annoyingly, it fitted him brilliantly.)

So, don't let your own **Kid Doubt** make you anxious about being normal. Ever. Again.

DARE TO
BE **YOU.**

# OVER TO YOU

## NORMAL NONSENSE

Can you think of any normal nonsense?

Are there any examples in your life of where there is a
**'ONE SIZE FITS ALL'** approach?

Think about your school, nearby shops and perhaps your local
sports club to start you off.

Why doesn't this approach make sense?

I'll give you an example to start you off. At my primary school, there
was only one size of chairs. The poor kids just starting at school
had to sit on seats that were huge. Their feet didn't even nearly
touch the floor, while the school-leavers were perilously close to
the ground with their knees around their ears. The chairs were
supposed to be good for everyone – but were actually comfortable
for no one.

BEING DIFFERENT

MAKES THE BIGGEST

DIFFERENCE

# 3

*They weren't a very good team. But they were our nearest club and we'd saved for the tickets. Emma had even rented her watch (it was quite swish) to a girl in our class for a week to bring in some extra money to spend on the day. We'd been looking forward to it for weeks.*

Saturday afternoon rolled around and we were ready. Personally, I thought the matching baseball caps were a bit much, but Emma was insistent. She said we looked like proper fans and she'd spent the last two weeks specially bending hers so it looked better on her head.

We were going to see Reading United play for the very first time. Neither of us had ever seen a professional team play before, but we had imagined it for years. It was going to be a great day. My dad dropped us off. We couldn't afford three tickets so he was going to listen to the match on the radio in the car park outside – if he could get a good enough signal. My dad was always on the lookout for a bargain and had taken the car (the one with **SYED BROTHERS**

painted on the side) to a dodgy car wash the month before. The engine had made a very weird noise ever since and the radio only worked if you parked the car in a north-facing direction.

So, there we were, in an actual football stadium. And after a brief row about whether to have a Coke or a Mountain Dew (only to find that the rent on Emma's watch didn't cover either – buying drinks at stadiums is extortionate!), the match was about to begin.

It started about ten minutes into the game. I didn't realise at first, it began quietly. I thought they were singing some song about the team. That's what happens at football matches, isn't it? Fans make up songs that don't quite rhyme about players on the other team. Or chant encouragement to their own team to the tune of something from *The Greatest Showman*. I almost tried to join in.

But then it got a bit louder and I realised. Slowly. That they weren't singing about the team – they were singing about me.

My dad is from Pakistan and so my skin colour is quite dark, like his. I'd never given it much thought until that moment. At the match I'd been dreaming of for years. The people around me started singing a song. A really horrible song. I won't repeat what the words were here, I think you'd be shocked. But the overall theme of it was that I looked different and so I didn't belong at the match.

I was so embarrassed, I didn't know where to look. I was ashamed, too, that my friend Emma had to listen to all of these people singing about me. What if she thought they were right? What if she changed her mind about me being one of her best friends? All of a sudden I was very glad she'd insisted on the baseball caps, and I pulled mine as far down across my face as I could manage. We left at half-time.

I didn't cry during the match, but I did that night. I couldn't understand how people could be so awful about something as meaningless as the colour of my skin. I was still the same person underneath, after all.

**Kid Doubt** really enjoyed that day though. Loved it, in fact. Happily watched as my anxiety grew and made me worried that I didn't fit in. I didn't go to watch a match again. For many, many years. I just couldn't. And I remember it often. People ask me, 'What football team do you support?' and I have to say no one. At that time, I didn't feel like I belonged at the match. So I couldn't possibly support a team.

This happened quite a long time ago. Things have changed and I think (and hope) that people today would know better than to sing such horrible songs. But that experience taught me what it was like to really feel like I didn't fit in – to feel different. What it feels like when you don't belong to the group. And it didn't feel good.

It doesn't matter what makes you feel different. It might be your skin, like me. Or your hair colour. Or that you like boys better than girls or girls better than boys. Or that you like chess not dance. Or that you prefer maths to nail varnish. Or that you have ADHD.

Or that your mum needs you to look after her. Or that you don't see your dad. Or that you don't have the same trainers as everyone else. I could go on for ever with this list. Seriously, I could.

But what if I could show you how **IMPORTANT** it is to be different? What if I could show you that the **BEST IDEAS** come from people who are different? What if I could show you that being different might make you **MORE SUCCESSFUL**?

That might be quite a boost, right? It would make us think twice before listening to **Kid Doubt**, at the very least.

So here goes.

Do you recognise any of these companies?

Yep, all massive. All make billions of pounds every year. Now, is there anything else they have in common? Let's look a little closer.

##  GOOGLE AND SERGEY BRIN

Sergey Brin invented Google. (I just googled Sergey Brin. Is that weird? To google the inventor of Google? I feel it might somehow break the space-time continuum.) His full name is Sergey Mikhaylovich Brin and he was born in Russia. He moved to the USA when he was six years old, after stints in Paris and Austria. At university he met Larry Page, and together they invented Google.

##  PEPSI AND INDRA NOOYI

Indra Nooyi was born in Chennai in India. Her family spoke Tamil as she grew up, and she spent her spare time playing cricket and performing in an all-girl rock band. She moved to the USA to study at a prestigious university called Yale, but when she graduated she had so little money that she went to her interviews in her Indian saris. She couldn't afford the suits she thought she was 'supposed' to wear. Until very recently she was the CEO (the boss) of Pepsi, and although she didn't found the company, she was responsible for many of their most successful initiatives (for example, buying healthier food brands). Pepsi's sales rose by 80 per cent during the twelve years that Indra Nooyi was in charge.

##  YAHOO! AND JERRY YANG

Jerry Yang founded the internet giant Yahoo!. When he was born in Taiwan, China, he was named Yang Chih-Yuan, but he moved to the USA when he was ten and adopted the name Jerry. His father had died and his mother went to live in California so that her extended family could help raise her two sons while she worked.

### WHEN HE ARRIVED IN AMERICA, YANG CHIH-YUAN COULD APPARENTLY ONLY SAY ONE ENGLISH WORD: 'SHOE'.

He invented Yahoo! with David Filo.

Do you see the connection? Yep. None of these hugely successful businesspeople were born in the USA. They were immigrants, and came to America after having lived in other countries. And while this is only a handful of examples, there are absolutely loads of similar ones. Research by the Kauffman Foundation has shown that you are **TWICE** as likely to start a new business if you are an immigrant.

Seriously? Can this be right? Why would being born somewhere else make any difference to whether you might start coding in your friend's garage and then invent one of the world's largest technology companies?

It comes down to this business of being **DIFFERENT**.

You see, immigrants have had different experiences, have grown up in a different culture, may speak a different language and may have parents with different beliefs to those common in their new country. Most importantly, they **KNOW** about changing things up. They've had to. It isn't easy arriving in a new country only being able to say the word 'shoe' (someone needs to ask Jerry Yang why he didn't learn 'Hello' as his one and only word). You have to be able to learn quickly, adapt and be flexible.

It is like a winning combination. Immigrants get the experience of changing things up when they move across the world **AND** they have a load of different ideas because they have lived in different places with parents and families with backgrounds from around the world.

No wonder these guys are great at thinking of new things.

# (((STAT ALERT!)))

Research done by the Center for American Entrepreneurship in 2017 shows that more than **HALF** of the top thirty-five companies in the USA were founded by immigrants or by the children of immigrants. If you zoom out to include the top 500 companies, the figure is 43 per cent. That is huge – especially when you consider that immigrants account for only about 14 per cent of the population of the USA overall.

These guys are really over-performing! **DIFFERENT IS THE NEW AWESOME.**

And guess what? You are also more likely to be an entrepreneur if you are dyslexic. Yep, that's right. Ever heard of Richard Branson, Lord Sugar, Ingvar Kamprad (he founded a teeny-weeny company called IKEA) or Jamie Oliver? All dyslexic. It turns out that having dyslexia makes you more likely to develop skills that are also super-useful when it comes to successfully running massive companies and having lots of people work for you. Skills like being brilliant at oral communication, thinking creatively and trusting others to do things for you. Seriously...

Now, I feel like I know what some of you are about to ask.

But what if I **WASN'T** born thousands of miles from here?! What if I was just born here and still live here? What does that mean? Will I not be successful because I'm not different enough? I haven't had to change countries, learn a different way of communicating and change my name to Jerry.

**WOW!** Well, this is a turn-up for the books! We've gone full circle – we used to be worried about being different. But now we're concerned

# WE MIGHT NOT BE DIFFERENT ENOUGH!

But don't worry. We are all **TOTALLY** different.

**DID YOU KNOW?**

Each of us literally lives in a different skin every few weeks. Apparently, humans shed 600,000 particles of skin **EVERY HOUR**. We must be living in a cloud of everyone else's skin. Yikes! Our skin cells renew themselves roughly every two to three weeks, which means right now you are living in a different skin to the one you were in three weeks ago.

# AND HOW DIFFERENT ARE WE FROM OTHER PEOPLE? VERY, AS IT TURNS OUT:

○ We all know about unique fingerprints. But did you know that everybody has a totally different **TONGUE** print as well? Don't secretly lick the tub of ice cream in the freezer. Everyone will know it was definitely you.

○ You can now buy a Mars bar (and anything else you fancy) not just with contactless credit cards but with your **FACE**. We all look so different to one another that we have designed technology that links your bank details to your face. Accidentally blink at the checkout and you could end up with a brand-new set of spoons!

We are all different. We look different. We like different things. Have different backgrounds. Have had different experiences. We all have so much to offer, if only we embrace those differences and stop trying to hide them.

If we can harness those differences and use them to our advantage, we are going to smash it. We might even change the world. And even better still, we won't waste energy trying to pretend we are the same as everyone else and getting upset when we don't manage it.

Think of it this way. Imagine this is you now:

**YOU.**

The size of the circle represents how much you know now.

As you practise stuff and learn new things, the circle will grow.

You in a few years' time. You've learned some more stuff, so your circle is bigger.

These are the cool kids at school:

**ZOE** She knows a lot.

**JAYDEN** He knows quite a bit, but a lot of what he knows is the same as what Zoe knows. He has been copying her for ages now, so their circles of knowledge overlap.

**PRIYA** She also knows quite a bit, but a lot of what she knows is the same as Zoe and Lily. She has been copying both of them.

**LILY** She doesn't know anything that Zoe doesn't already know. She sits next to Zoe. They chat all of the time. Lily wants to be exactly like Zoe. And she has been copying Priya too, so her circle is completely inside Zoe's.

Now imagine that the circle below represents where all of the great ideas, inventions and brilliant breakthroughs out there could possibly come from. Let's call it...

# THE WORLD OF GOOD IDEAS.

Let's put the cool kids in **The World of Good Ideas**.

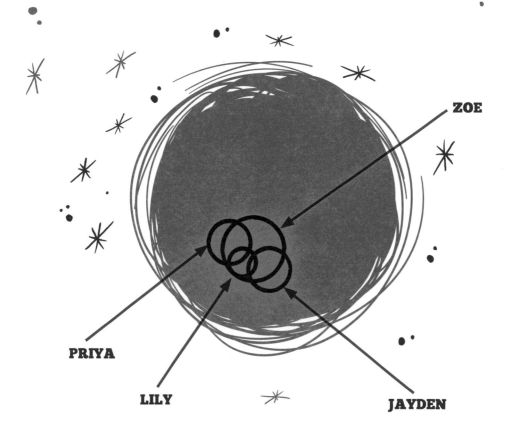

Now, the cool kids have clearly got some good ideas between them. Everyone has. But because they have spent so long trying to copy each other, making sure they fit in, they've become **CLONES** of each other.

Lily doesn't have any ideas that Zoe doesn't already have. Poor Lily. She thinks she is super-cool because she is copying Zoe, but in reality she has kind of reduced her ability to think of new ways of doing things. She isn't likely to see the world as changeable, or to try and forge her own path. Because she wants her path to be exactly like Zoe's and quite a lot like Priya's.

So ask yourself: where would you like to be in
**The World of Good Ideas**?

# OPTION 1

In Option 1, you are in with the cool kids but you haven't really got many new ideas of your own. In Option 2 you are harnessing the fact that you are **PROUD** of your differences. You have loads of new and interesting ideas based on the different background you have. Based on the fact that you like different stuff. Based on the fact that you think differently. Based on the fact that your family is different so you have had different experiences.

# OPTION 2

While the cool kids are all having the same ideas, in Option 2, **YOU** are the one who could come up with a different view that might change the world.

Imagine you wanted to make up a team for a class project made up of the most creative people from the diagram in Option 2. You'd choose you and Zoe, wouldn't you? All the other kids think the same as Zoe, so they aren't needed in the team.

In fact, the ideal, best and most creative
team might look a bit like this:

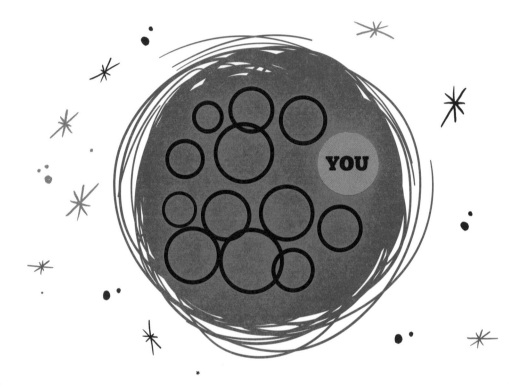

Here, **The World of Good Ideas** is almost completely covered
by different people with different views. This team is going to be
awesome at problem-solving because they will be able to come up
with the greatest number of possible solutions. They are not clones
of each other. They aren't copycats. This team might have people
from different backgrounds, people with different favourite foods,
people with different ideas, people with neurodiversity. They are
proud of their differences and understand why thinking differently
is so important.

There are loads of things that might make you feel different. Whatever it is, embrace it.

# IN A WORLD THAT NEEDS GOOD IDEAS, IT IS YOUR GREATEST STRENGTH.

# 'I HAVE ASPERGER'S, AND THAT MEANS I'M SOMETIMES A BIT DIFFERENT FROM THE NORM. GIVEN THE RIGHT CIRCUMSTANCES, BEING DIFFERENT IS A SUPERPOWER.'

GRETA THUNBERG, ECO-ACTIVIST EXTRAORDINAIRE

# NON-CONFORMING NOBELS

A Nobel Prize is kind of a big deal, right? Bigger even than winning the Czech Open table-tennis competition. (I have only won one of the two. I'll leave you to guess which.)

Anyway, winning a Nobel Prize is a massive deal. They are given for outstanding contributions to humanity. It really doesn't get bigger than this. They are awarded in Chemistry, Physics, Medicine, Literature, Economics and Peace, and you basically have to have actually changed the world in order to get one.

A group of fifteen researchers at Michigan State University in the USA had a look into everyone in each Nobel Prize category who had won between 1901 and 2005. And they compared them to the other brilliant experts who were around at the same time, but who didn't win.

What they found was quite amazing.

They found that the people who won the Nobel Prizes were much more likely to have a hobby or an interest in the 'arts' (so art, music, painting, poetry, dancing, sculpting, that type of thing) than the experts who didn't win.

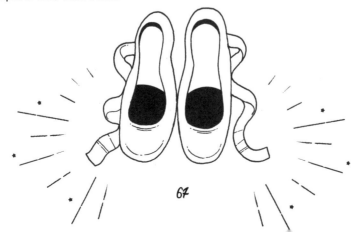

Check out the results of their research …

2 x more likely to win

Experts who also like playing a musical instrument or conducting

7.5 x more likely to win

Experts who also like crafts, woodwork, electronics or glass-blowing

Experts who also like drawing, painting and sculpting

7 x more likely to win

Experts who also like performing, dancing or doing magic

22 x more likely to win

Experts who also like writing poetry, plays or stories

12 x more likely to win

So if I take up the clarinet and then paint a piece of woodwork while dancing to a piece of my own poetry, am I basically guaranteed a Nobel? Well, I'd have to get very good at physics or chemistry or medicine first, which might take a while. Still, it's all looking much more promising than it was ten minutes ago.

But there is a serious point here. Why is this happening? Why is an expert much more likely to win a Nobel Prize if they have an artistic hobby?

I'm guessing that, by now, you already know the answer.

It is because these experts are **DIFFERENT.** Take the creative scientists, for example. They don't spend all of their time with other scientists who might all think in a very similar way. Instead, they have an outside interest in which they build new skills, develop new ideas and meet new people. They connect these 'outsider' ideas to their scientific work, making it more likely that they will come up with even better ideas than other scientists. And then, when they do, this idea changes humanity and they win the **NOBEL PRIZE**.

I am a bit different. I am the son of an immigrant. And my dad wasn't ever afraid of change. Aged 20, he was a Muslim man living in Pakistan. Aged 22, he was a Christian man living in Kent, UK. That's quite a lot of change! He taught me not to listen to anyone who talked down to me because I was different. He taught me to work hard, take control and go out and forge my own path.

You can do it too.

# BEING DIFFERENT REALLY IS AWESOME.

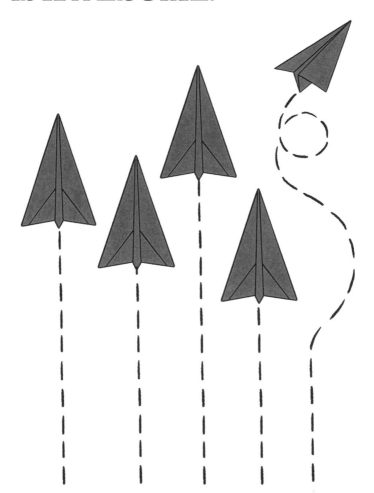

# OVER TO YOU

## STRENGTH IN DIFFERENCES

Take a piece of paper and write the words **MY STRENGTHS**
at the top.

Underneath, write a list of all the ways that you are different to
other people. Make a huge list if you like. As long as you can!

Next to each one, write down how this difference could be useful
to you now or in the future.

If you're looking at the list and feeling like maybe you could do
with new inspiration, try thinking about the following:

○ **COULD YOU BE MORE OPEN TO**
## NEW THINGS AND NEW IDEAS?

○ **IS THERE TIME TO FIT IN A**
## NEW HOBBY, SOMETHING THAT
## NO ONE ELSE YOU KNOW DOES?

# 4

*It's time, I think. I might need a minute to collect my thoughts, but I reckon I am just about ready to tell you about the Syed family car. It was a blue Peugeot Talbot Samba. Nothing unusual there, you might think.*

Oh, but did I mention that it happened to have **SYED BROTHERS** emblazoned in bright orange paint along the side?

We've already learned that there is no such thing as normal. And that was **DEFINITELY** the case with that car. It was one of a kind.

It all started when my dad (who is honestly a terrible driver, but please don't tell him I said that) crashed our car into the local bus station. That is not easy to do, I can tell you. Mum couldn't understand how my dad had failed to notice the eighteen purple double-deckers parked up next to a massive two-storey building. But he hadn't.

It was a bad day in the Syed house: Dad was in a huge mood, and now the car (which wasn't great to start with) had an imprint of the bus station down one side. So, we needed a new car. But we couldn't really afford one – which was why my dad was in a huge mood.

Now, this situation (yes, let's call it a situation. It definitely was one) happened around the same time as the height of the obsession my brother and I had with a footballer called…Kevin Keegan.

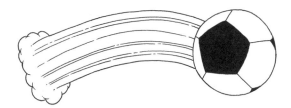

## COPYING KEVIN

Kev was **AMAZING**. Unbelievable. Incredible. We thought he was the most fantastic player we had ever seen. It wasn't just us either, a lot of other people thought so too. He was the captain of England and he just worked **SO** hard. If you saw him on the pitch, you couldn't quite believe the energy he had. He was everywhere! He scored goals (loads of them), he helped other players score goals and he stopped the opposition scoring goals. It was like he was able to do absolutely everything.

And my brother and I wanted to be just like him. **EXACTLY** like him.

Now, we were obviously training hard at table tennis. Which we loved. We were getting pretty good at it too. But we did also love football, and with the exception of the time I wanted to read *The Hobbit* (but **Kid Doubt** put a swift end to my confidence to do that), we played it every breaktime. When we did, I was always Kevin Keegan – in my head, obviously. I even wrote 'Kevin' on the inside of my football boots in permanent marker and a small (well, I thought it was small until my mum saw it from 100 metres away and went mad) number seven on my school jumper. Seven was Kevin's number when he played for England.

My brother and I had posters of Kevin on our wall. We tried to watch Kevin play on TV all the time. And when it came to getting the new car, we wanted the same one that Kevin had. That's how it all started.

To this day, I have no idea what car Kevin Keegan actually owned. But suffice to say, it was **NOT** that likely that the Syeds were going to be able to afford the same one. My mum worked in the local supermarket and my dad taught accounting at the nearby university. The budget for a Ferrari or a Porsche was, frankly, non-existent. But that didn't stop us trying to convince Dad that we really **MUST** have the same kind of car that Kevin had. I found a picture of something called an 'executive limousine' in a magazine at school that I cut out and left on Dad's bed. It looked like the kind of car Kevin would drive. Dad's mood got worse.

At the time, we couldn't understand why. But looking back, I am starting to suspect it was something to do with us going on about Kevin's car and the fact that our own car was no longer roadworthy . . .

Now, let's take a moment and have a think about this situation with Kevin. On the surface, it might just seem like a funny story (you can be the judge of that) about a bus station and an obsession with Kevin Keegan. But underneath that, there is quite a big bit of science lurking about the way we have evolved as humans. This is **BIG** stuff. And it explains why we seem to be so keen to copy other people. Why we want to be like famous people or people we think of as successful.

# THIS IS REALLY BIG STUFF.

You'd probably agree that if you want to be a great footballer, it makes sense to think of some actual great footballers and try to work out what they have been doing to get so great. You'd probably therefore also agree that copying Kevin's attitude to training by turning up and trying your very hardest might be a good idea. And practising the goal-scoring skills that Kevin deployed so well might also be useful in getting good at football.

We did all of that. We did get to training early. We did practise the skills we witnessed when we watched him. So far, so good.

## BUT.

This is where the weird bit happens. Our copying of Kevin didn't stop there. It seemed to know no bounds.

As a superstar footballer, Kevin also appeared in adverts and was the 'face' of quite a few products. Here is a list of some of them:

**The Kevin Keegan Ice Lolly (seriously)**
The lolly stick in the middle was a mini-replica of Kevin Keegan.

**Brut aftershave and shower gel**
A very strong-smelling series of shower-based products.

**Smiths Crisps**
Delicious.

**The Grundig 400**
A very old version of a radio, in case you were wondering (which I suspect you were).

**Sugar Puffs**
A breakfast cereal. A very sugary one. Each portion back then had two cubes of sugar. Unclear if Kevin ever ate any actual Puffs.

And here is the thing. We wanted it **ALL**. Everything. The lot.

Dad wouldn't buy the radio, he said it was too expensive. But we persuaded Mum to let us have Sugar Puffs on Saturdays as a treat and, if we ever saw the ice lollies on sale, it was a race to see who could eat them first to get down to the Keegan-shaped lolly stick. The Brut collection is a whole other story. My brother went all the way to the Boots in town on the bus and spent six months' worth of his pocket money on some Brut aftershave. He didn't even shave yet and he had no clue where to spray it.

Kevin released a song too. It was called 'Head Over Heels in Love'. And despite the disappointment of not owning Kevin's Grundig 400 radio and therefore not hearing the song as often as we might have liked, we still learned all of the words.

## WHAT ON EARTH WERE WE THINKING?

Why **WERE** we doing this? Why would eating a lolly with a Kevin-shaped stick, or owning a Grundig 400, have made us better footballers? It wouldn't. Why would spraying a dubiously strong perfume somewhere (we weren't sure where) while singing a seriously bad love song make us suddenly able to score goals? It just wouldn't.

We wanted what Kevin had. So we wanted anything he put his name to. For years!

## But WHY?

# THE SCIENCE BIT

Joseph Henrich is a professor at Harvard University (which is a seriously good place for learning in the USA). And he has got a theory about all of this. One I reckon we should have a proper think about. He thinks humans have a tendency to **OVER-COPY** or **OVER-IMITATE** people we think are successful.

You see, when we are young, we learn things by copying adults or other children who are older than us. But Professor Henrich thinks that rather than spending ages figuring out which exact bits of their actions we should copy if we want to be good at a certain thing, we find it easier just to copy absolutely everything.

Humans are complicated after all, and it would take us a really, really long time to learn anything if we first needed to work out which bits were the right ones to copy. So instead, we over-copy and copy **THE LOT**. That way, we figure we've got all our bases covered and we'll definitely nail whatever it is we are trying to learn.

Take an example. You're a two-year-old and you want to learn how to use a spoon. You've seen your mum and your older sister do it but you're not totally sure what makes them really good at getting the yoghurt out of the pot and into their mouths neatly. You, the two-year-old, get yoghurt everywhere. So what do you do?

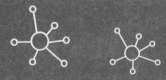

Professor Henrich reckons that instead of spending ages thinking about which bit of your mum's actions make her really brilliant at using a spoon, you just copy everything she does. Because if you do that, you'll end up copying the right bits eventually and you're sure to perfect the spoon/yoghurt/mouth skill. Rather than ending lunch with yoghurt smeared across your face, your eyes and the chair, like you usually do.

But the decision to copy everything means that you start copying a load of stuff that has **NOTHING** to do with using a spoon. You might start to copy your mum picking up the spoon (useful, because that is to do with the spoon). But you might also start copying her smile (nothing to do with the spoon) or the tone of her voice (nothing to do with the spoon) or you might steal her lipstick and try putting it on like she does (nothing to do with the spoon). In the end you might also copy the way your mum turns the spoon towards her when she's about to put it into her mouth (useful, definitely to do with the spoon).

You see? You've copied everything she does, and eventually you copied all the right bits to help with the spoon business – but along with a load of other stuff too.

OUR INSTINCT TO OVER-COPY IS A POWERFUL ONE. IT **HELPS US TO LEARN**, BUT IT ALSO MEANS WE END UP **COPYING** A LOAD OF **BEHAVIOUR** THAT IS TOTALLY **USELESS** TO US.

This is what was going on with me, my brother and Kevin Keegan. While we were copying some of things that made Kevin a great footballer (like his training and ball skills), we were also copying the aftershave we thought he wore and the breakfast cereal we thought he ate and wanting the radio we thought he listened to.

Copying to learn is a great idea. Over-copying when we are a bit older is, well, about as useful as aftershave when you don't even shave. And that is exactly why companies get famous people to advertise their products.

Did you know that Beyoncé was paid millions to advertise Pepsi? She is an incredible performer, so it's no surprise that people want to be successful just like she is. And when her fans copy her hard work, they might try some singing lessons – but they are **ALSO** likely to over-copy and start buying cans of Pepsi because they are told on TV that Beyoncé likes Pepsi.

But is drinking a can of Pepsi what makes Beyoncé one of the best performers in the world? Highly. Unlikely. So if you did want to be the next person to headline Glastonbury, would drinking Pepsi be of any help? Highly. Unlikely. But we over-copy and buy the Pepsi anyway. Because we are maniacs with all the copying.

It's not that we always do this deliberately. A lot of this copying madness is going on at the back of our brains without us even noticing. But now that we know about it, we can pay attention and do something about it. Maybe we should really question who we are copying. And more importantly, question **WHAT** it is about that person we are copying.

## WHO ARE WE COPYING?

It is perfectly logical to try and copy things about people that you truly admire. Copying Malala's bravery and courage would be a perfectly sensible thing to do. Copying her choice of shoes, her gym schedule or whether she follows a vegetarian diet? Nope. Probably not going to make you an international ambassador for peace across the world.

Copying Ed Sheeran's commitment to practising his guitar would be a great idea if you want to play the guitar. But spending an absolute fortune on a designer checked shirt just like his? Nope. Not likely to help much in the musical talent department.

Now that we are aware of our (massive) tendency to over-copy, maybe we can take a moment to pause. To stop and think hard about the people we are copying on TV, on social media, on YouTube or even at school. You see, this over-copying makes us want to copy the cool kids at school too. To copy the things they do, to wear the same things they do. We think they are successful. They're cool right, so they must be? So we should copy them? Wrong. So the next time **Kid Doubt** is sneering at you and making you anxious that you don't have the latest smartphone or that your trainers are not as cool as everyone else's, think seriously about what is really going on. Are those things truly going to help you reach your goals?

Be yourself. Copy the traits in people you admire that are likely to be good for you. Like kindness, hard work and courage.

Question yourself if you are copying other things. Things that make no difference to **YOUR** success. Things **YOU** don't really believe in. Things that **YOU** don't even like. Don't try to (over)copy someone else's life.

**NOW, I GUESS WE SHOULD FINISH THE STORY OF OUR NEW CAR …**

Dad went out to collect it one Saturday morning. We had a school football match and he said he'd pick us up in it. We thought we were going to be driving back home in style. Just like Kevin would drive home from a match.

It turned out to be the shock of a lifetime.

When my dad arrived, we couldn't quite believe it. I can still feel the horror sweep over me as I write this. The car was tiny, nothing like Kevin's (or what we imagined Kevin's would have been like). And it had the words **SYED BROTHERS** painted in enormous bright orange writing. **ON BOTH SIDES.**

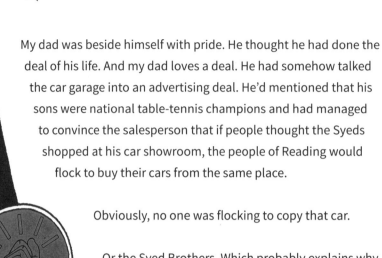

My dad was beside himself with pride. He thought he had done the deal of his life. And my dad loves a deal. He had somehow talked the car garage into an advertising deal. He'd mentioned that his sons were national table-tennis champions and had managed to convince the salesperson that if people thought the Syeds shopped at his car showroom, the people of Reading would flock to buy their cars from the same place.

Obviously, no one was flocking to copy that car.

Or the Syed Brothers. Which probably explains why (unlike Beyoncé, who got millions from Pepsi) my dad only got a very small discount on the price of a Peugeot Talbot Samba.

But there it was. For all to see. For the

# NEXT

# SEVEN

# YEARS.

# OVER TO YOU

## CLONE WARS

○ Think of someone you admire. It could be someone famous or someone in your family or someone at school.

○ Write down all of the things you might be inclined to copy about that person. (Their hard work? Their training schedule? Their commitment to helping other people? Their lipstick? Their trainers?)

○ Now ask yourself: of all of those things, which ones are truly going to make a difference in helping you to achieve your own goals?

THE THING I ADMIRE ABOUT YOU IS ...

*Wow. We have already covered **A LOT**. You know that one size definitely does **NOT** fit all of us because you are unique. You know that your differences are your greatest strength. **AND** you now know all about that car, and the over-copying.*

So I am hoping that you are already feeling a bit more confident when you see or hear your **Kid Doubt**. But we are not finished yet! Nope. We have a load more strategies to deploy in our effort to banish him.

So, let's not wait around. Let's get to it.

I need to tell you about when I got my first job. Actually, my second job. My first job was a short affair that ended badly. It involved helping my mum's friend to move house and a smashed china parrot. Let's just say, I haven't been involved in the home removals business since.

Anyway, back to the other one.

I had been playing table tennis for quite a few years, but I was beginning to realise that my career as the world's twentieth-best table-tennis player wasn't going to last for ever. I was getting a little older and my legs

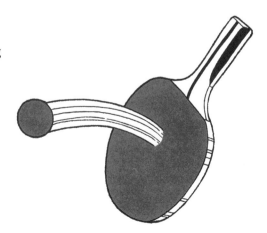

were just not as lightning-quick as they once had been. It was a bit disappointing, but it was something I had known would happen. Still, it was scary trying to figure out what I was going to do with the rest of my life.

My next best career idea involved Kevin Keegan. I wanted to play football with him. But sadly, his legs weren't as quick as they had once been either, and he had stopped playing too. So it looked like athletic options were out.

Now, I really liked writing. Loved it, in fact. I had submitted a few short articles for the local newspaper and wondered whether there was any small chance that I might be able to write for my next job. But **Kid Doubt** was back and I'd forgotten **The Plan** (remember **The Plan**? The manifesto for being **ME**?). I started to listen to the voice in my head saying things like:

IS ANYONE REALLY GOING TO WANT TO READ WHAT YOU WRITE, AN EX-PING-PONG PLAYER WITH NO EXPERIENCE OF WRITING? AND HOW ON EARTH WOULD YOU BE ABLE TO PHONE UP A NEWSPAPER EDITOR AND ASK IF THEY WOULD GIVE YOU A JOB. WHAT ON EARTH WOULD YOU SAY?

So I shelved that idea. I put aside my dream of being a writer and got a job in an office.

Don't get me wrong, it was a really great job. One I was lucky to get and one that a lot of people wanted. It was with a huge bank in the centre of London. It had revolving doors and a silver fountain in the entrance with real fish in. I couldn't quite believe that they actually wanted me to work there (**Kid Doubt** again!).

My table-tennis coach said it was 'the opportunity of a lifetime'. My dad kept telling me that this bank was where the 'movers and shakers' worked.

My brother thought we had hit the big time. The pay was good and he was certain that this job was going to 'make us rich'. I wasn't sure about the 'us' bit as he was clearly not going to be doing the actual work, but nonetheless I was pleased that he seemed so proud of me (for once).

Everyone thought that this job was the best thing ever. Except me. I didn't want the job. I tried to, but it just didn't motivate me in the same way that table tennis once had. Still, I decided to take it. I didn't want to let everyone down. I had forgotten that I was supposed to be making choices that were right for **ME**.

**I HAD FORGOTTEN THE PLAN.**

When I got there, I didn't see that many people moving or shaking. I saw a lot of people working super-hard in jobs they seemed to enjoy.

But I just didn't love it like they did.

After a while at the bank, I remembered **The Plan**. I built up some courage and called my dad. I told him that this job wasn't for me. I told him that I had given it my best shot, I had tried hard but I just knew it wasn't the right fit. I was worried. I thought he was going to tell me that I wasn't a 'mover', let alone a 'shaker'. That he'd be annoyed that I was giving up on a job that could genuinely have made me a millionaire.

But he wasn't. He told me to follow my dream. And I've never looked back.

We'll come back to the story of the job a bit later. But I want to pause right here for a minute. Because something important happened the day I phoned my dad. Something that I think is going to help you when you are figuring out your own path. When you want to **DARE TO BE YOU**.

- ○ I questioned whether the job was **RIGHT** for **ME**.
- ○ I questioned whether there was something that would be **BETTER FOR ME**.
- ○ I questioned whether I could **MAKE A CHANGE**.

And as it turns out, having the confidence to question what is happening around you and an ability to be flexible as things change are going to be two of the most important skills you can have for the future.

# LET'S BE READY TO MAKE A CHANGE

You've probably noticed that things are changing in the world around us. A lot. And fast! Some people think that things are changing at the fastest rate we have ever seen in history. New technology is being developed every minute of every day. We can connect with literally millions of people at the touch of a button – even grandparents got the hang of chatting via Zoom once the coronavirus lockdowns started. We have access to information on any topic we could possibly imagine.

**INCREDIBLE INNOVATIONS:**

O The radio took 38 years to reach fifty million listeners after it had been invented. The TV took thirteen years to reach fifty million viewers. It took the internet four years to reach fifty million users. It took Facebook less than two years – and it took Pokémon Go just nineteen days.

O There are 5,600,000,000 searches on Google every day. That is two hundred times more than twenty years ago. And (you'll hardly believe this) there was actually a time before Google even existed. How on earth did we find anything out?

O We have invented tiny cameras that are the size of a pill. They can be swallowed so they can photograph your insides and allow doctors to see what is going on inside your tummy and beyond. (Those trillion micro-organisms in your intestines might get their own moment on social media! Eww…)

O The UK Space agency has announced plans to launch an aeroplane capable of taking passengers to New York in one hour and Australia in just four hours. You could actually go to Bondi Beach for lunch and come home in time for dinner!

- Virgin Galactic is about to take its first tourists into space. Is this the beginning of holidays on Mars?

And we have started to invent robots. Not the kind you see in sci-fi movies that roam around destroying the human race, but ones that can actually do quite a lot of useful things. You may even have used one. Amazon's Alexa, for example. She can tell jokes, order your shopping and tell you what the weather will be like a week on Wednesday.

# ((( INTERESTING FACT ALERT )))

*Do you know why Amazon called Alexa, Alexa? Because they wanted a name with an X in it. Apparently it is easier for their software to detect people saying the letter X even if they mumble! I do worry about confusion in houses where there is an Amazon Alexa and a person called Alexa. There could be some terrible mix-ups.*

Google is working on cars that will drive themselves. How great will that be? Amazing. It can't come soon enough for the Syed family. My dad needs one as soon as possible, he is a terrible driver. (Did I mention he once caused a four-car pile-up in the queue at a McDonalds drive-through?) Just think about how much easier self-driving cars will be. People can kick back and do other things in the car. Plus they will likely be safer and reduce crashes and will probably be much better for the environment too.

But here is the thing. These fancy new cars won't be great for everyone. For example, they won't be that great for taxi drivers. Or anyone who wants to be a taxi driver.

We might soon have robots diagnosing our medical ailments. They'll be able to flick through a library of symptoms, scans and the latest research in a matter of milliseconds, providing an accurate diagnosis and treatment faster than you can say

**MY HEAD HURTS.**

Amazing!

Although what are the doctors going to do then?

Robots are packing the stuff we order online. Soon they'll be delivering it. Maybe by drone. Awesome!

But what about the packers and post people? What are they going to do when this technology arrives?

Some estimates predict that by 2060, robots might be able to do almost all of the jobs that we know of today. So what on earth are humans going to do then? That is the issue. What **ARE** we going to do?

Well, we are going to have to get prepped and ready to do jobs that maybe haven't even been invented yet.

I know what you are going to say. **HOW ON EARTH** do we prepare for that? You just said these jobs haven't even been invented yet! What am I supposed to prep?!

Well, we should prep our …

And I don't mean hot-foot it to the nearest yoga class. I mean that we should get comfortable with changing things up. Because that is what we are going to have to do in the future. And often.

We need to make sure that we are happy to **QUESTION** things, that we are **CURIOUS** to find better ways of doing things and that we are **ADAPTABLE** when we need to make changes.

# LET'S CHANGE OUR ATTITUDE TO CHANGE

Change can sometimes be daunting. When the things we have become used to start to look different, **Kid Doubt** can be right in there making us worried that we won't be able to cope.

But in truth, change is not something we should be fearful of. We just need to be ready. After all, it's not like it hasn't happened before. The coronavirus pandemic is a recent example. A really tough time that has affected the whole world in so many different ways. It has caused difficulties for millions of people. But it has also offered a chance to think differently about the way we live our lives. To think differently about the way we work, the way we communicate and the way we care for each other. Think of these other head-spinning changes that people have had to adapt to throughout history...

##  MONEY BAGS

We haven't always used money. Until as late as the thirteenth century, most of us lived in the countryside and swapped things that we had or we made. For example, you could swap your cow for two sheep, if you needed some sheep. If you didn't, you might swap your cow's milk for someone else's carrots. But as more of us moved to towns, all of this swapping got quite tricky. Cows were bulky (not to mention messy) things to keep in a one-bedroom flat in town. And what if you wanted some carrots but the carrot-seller didn't want your milk? So we started to use money and coins as a method of exchange instead.

##  CENTRE OF THE UNIVERSE

We used to think the Sun revolved around the Earth! We had to have a serious rethink when Copernicus discovered the exact opposite was going on in 1543. There was a whole lot of new physics to be done after that.

## ⭐ BRIGHT SPARKS

Electricity is a relatively recent thing – the first proper lightbulbs weren't really used until 1882. Imagine if we hadn't been flexible and adaptable and ready for that change? We'd be living in very dark houses, cooking over a smoky fire and washing our clothes in the bath while most definitely not watching anything on YouTube.

## ⭐ RING-RING

We didn't always have telephones, either. It wasn't until 1876 that the first patent for a telephone was registered. And I don't mean mobile telephones where you can take the thing with you anywhere and talk and text and game and shop and selfie (all at the same time). The first telephones were huge and had cords that were fixed to a wall. Before that, we couldn't talk to each other at all unless we were actually standing in the same room. If you wanted to meet someone, you'd have to write to them and ask them to see you three weeks next Thursday. And you couldn't cancel or be late. You wouldn't be able to tell them you weren't coming!

#  PLASTIC (NOT SO) FANTASTIC

Plastic was first invented in 1907. It was cheap, durable and lightweight, and wow, did we go mad for it. We got carried away without thinking about whether it was good for our planet or our ocean life. The stuff is seriously difficult to get rid of when you don't want it any more. So, even though we got used to a world filled with plastic, now we've decided to try to make a change and ditch it. We've got a long way to go on this one, but you know what? We've coped so far. We've found that it **IS** possible to drink from a paper straw, and that, in fact, most people can lean down the extra 4 cm and just drink from the actual cup. We've realised that we don't need 27 new plastic shopping bags each time we go to the supermarket – we can reuse one or two made out of cotton.

All of these changes have one thing in common. They were brought about by people who looked at the world around them, scratched their heads, and thought to question if there was a better way of doing things. When we ask questions, we can change the world.

# QUIZZICAL KIDS

According to a piece of research led by psychologist Dr Sam Wass, young children ask a mega 73 questions every single day. Apparently our curiosity is at its maximum when we are just four years old! That's when we are asking the most questions.

You see, at four years old we are too young to be worried about **Kid Doubt**. We may not have even met him yet! We are just genuinely interested in learning about the world around us. Figuring out the answers that we are going to need to forge our own path. We aren't thinking about fitting in, being normal or what hairstyle looks best. We aren't ashamed to ask questions in case we look stupid.

But somewhere along the line, we start to question things less often. We begin to think that things aren't to be questioned. We forget **The Plan**.

Keep questioning. Keep asking. Keep curious.

Here are two brave individuals who have been bold enough to ask questions in pursuit of making their world a better place.

## MALALA YOUSAFZAI

Malala was born in Pakistan in 1997. When she was just 11, the Taliban took control of the village in which she lived. The extremists banned girls from going to school. They didn't believe girls needed an education.

Malala wasn't happy simply to accept these new rules. She passionately believed in the rights of girls to go to school. So she decided to speak out and question the policies of the Taliban.

Sadly, Malala was attacked for questioning the Taliban. She was transferred to the UK for treatment for her injuries. She's never regretted it though.

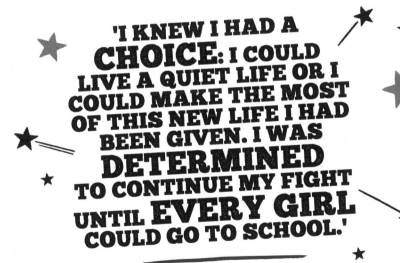

'I KNEW I HAD A CHOICE: I COULD LIVE A QUIET LIFE OR I COULD MAKE THE MOST OF THIS NEW LIFE I HAD BEEN GIVEN. I WAS DETERMINED TO CONTINUE MY FIGHT UNTIL EVERY GIRL COULD GO TO SCHOOL.'

Malala now attends Oxford University, but she remains passionate every single day about campaigning for girls' right to attend school.

## GRETA THUNBERG

Born in Stockholm in 2003, Greta Thunberg learned about the issues our climate faces when she was eight years old. She couldn't understand why there wasn't more being done about it.

She decided that she was going to ask that question. And she has. She has called upon governments all over the world to take action.

'WE CAN'T SAVE THE WORLD BY PLAYING BY THE RULES, BECAUSE THE RULES HAVE TO BE CHANGED. EVERYTHING NEEDS TO CHANGE - AND IT HAS TO START TODAY.'

She inspired Fridays for Future, a school climate strike movement, and more than a million students around the globe have participated.

# DON'T HOLD BACK

If we want to make things work for us, and if we want to find out if we can change things around us, we need to be prepared to ask questions. To muscle in front of **Kid Doubt**, put our nerves to one side, and put our hands up. So be brave. Have the courage to see if there is a way that things could work better.

So don't be afraid to ask. If you never do, you'll always wonder what the answer might have been.

**BUT.**

Here's the thing.

## ONCE YOU HAVE THE ANSWER, UNLESS YOU ACTUALLY ACT ON IT

### ... UNLESS YOU TAKE CONTROL AND MAKE A CHANGE...

## NOTHING. IS. GOING. TO. BE. DIFFERENT.

So the next step in **DARING TO BE YOU** is making sure we know how to take some action. After all, it was painting maestro Pablo Picasso who said:

ACTION IS THE KEY TO ALL SUCCESS.

YOUR FUTURE

# OVER TO YOU

## CURIOUSER AND CURIOUSER

It can be daunting to think about making your own change. But let's break it down like this. Here is my own example. What would you have in your list?

### WHAT CAN I DEFINITELY CHANGE?

My socks each morning.

How hard I try at something. There's a great book about that I think? Called something to do with Awesome?

What I do or don't decide to copy from other people. I've stopped singing Kevin's hit song now. And I definitely wouldn't follow anyone to a bakery with matches any more.

### WHAT DO I THINK I CAN'T CHANGE - BUT MAYBE IF I'M BRAVE ENOUGH TO QUESTION IT, I CAN?

How quickly my maths teacher used to go in class. I didn't realise until years afterwards that she would have happily slowed down or given me some extra help. I didn't ask back then, but I wish I had.

The office job. It wasn't for me. I'd love to see if I could try writing. Could I?

*Be brave and focus on these!*

### WHAT CAN I DEFINITELY NOT CHANGE?

My brother and how competitive he is.

What happened yesterday.

The weather. No point complaining it's cold. That won't make it any warmer.

My friends if they don't like me for who I am. Tim Preston and Philip Beck and the bakery crew were just not worth trying to impress.

Take charge. Ask the questions. **You can do it.**

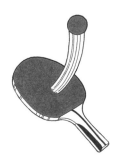

# 6

*I kick myself sometimes. Well, I don't actually because that would hurt. But I **ALMOST** had one of the best inventions of the century. **ALMOST**. But almost is as good as not having had it at all.*

There is a lot of kit associated with table tennis. You might not think it, but there is. There's bats (I'd usually have about five of them at any one time), there's balls (I'd have about fifty of them), there's special shoes, tracksuits (I love a tracksuit), T-shirts, shorts and socks. And glue. Literally loads of glue. I bet that's one you didn't see coming. Did you know that table-tennis players are brilliant at arts and crafts?

∘ ∘ ∘ ∘ ∘ ∘ ∘ ∘ ∘ ∘ ∘ ∘ ∘ ∘ ∘ ∘ ∘ ∘ ∘ ∘ ∘ ∘ ∘ ∘ ∘ ∘ ∘ ∘ ∘

*Actually, this is interesting, and very relevant to all the stuff we talked about in chapter five. So stick with me (get it?). Have you ever thought about the rubber stuff on either side of a table-tennis bat? Probably not. But guess what? **IT IS CHANGEABLE!** You don't have to use the rubber that the bat comes with. You can take it off and replace it with different textured rubber that suits your style of play better. So in my day, table-tennis players used to carry sheets of rubber that they cut into bat-shaped circles and glued on to their bats. Before every match! There were even special rooms just for gluing and sticking at every tournament. So, question things. You might be able to glue on something different. That works better for **YOU**.*

∘ ∘ ∘ ∘ ∘ ∘ ∘ ∘ ∘ ∘ ∘ ∘ ∘ ∘ ∘ ∘ ∘ ∘ ∘ ∘ ∘ ∘ ∘ ∘ ∘ ∘ ∘ ∘ ∘

But back to the time I nearly had the best invention of the century. It was while I was carrying **ALL THIS KIT** around. I had a huge blue sports holdall. It had two handles and a shoulder strap. And what with all the clean kit, the spare bats and last week's kit that I hadn't bothered to empty out, it was **VERY** heavy.

My shoulder hurt when I carried it. And I carried it everywhere. To France, to Sweden, to Japan. It got stolen on the way to Bergen, Norway, but that is a whole other story. Anyway, it was a (heavy) nightmare.

And I used to think to myself:

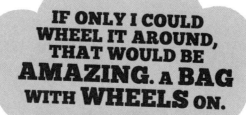

IF ONLY I COULD WHEEL IT AROUND, THAT WOULD BE **AMAZING.** A BAG WITH **WHEELS** ON.

# **OMG!** I HAD INVENTED THE SUITCASE ON WHEELS!

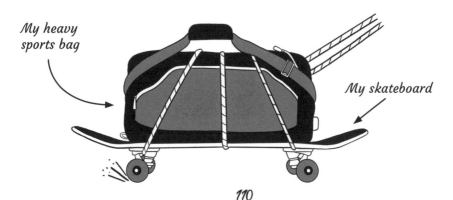

My heavy sports bag

My skateboard

And believe it or not, that hadn't been invented when I was young. But the thing is . . . I hadn't actually invented it. Because I just thought of it, in my mind. And stopped there. **Kid Doubt** was around, you see. He was saying it was a rubbish idea. He was saying that he thought other people might laugh at me if I attached the skateboard I was still carrying round to the bottom of the bag. And I listened to him.

You can think about this whole business of making change as a series of steps. I think there are three of them. In this case, I had done Step 1 and Step 2:

## STEP 1: ASK THE QUESTION.

I had questioned the problem – could anything be done about my heavy bag?

## STEP 2: THINK OF A SOLUTION.

I had thought of the solution – put wheels on the bag.

## STEP 3: ACT ON IT.

Make it happen – put the wheels on the bag.

. . . Nope, I didn't do step 3.

I DIDN'T DO ANYTHING ABOUT IT!

I just carried on lugging the bag to each tournament. Straining myself with each and every journey.

It is impossible now to think of a world where suitcases didn't have wheels. But that is how it used to be. It took centuries for someone to connect the problem of heavy suitcases to the solution of the wheel. That could have been me. Instead it was a chap called Bernard Sadow, who came up with the idea while struggling with some heavy suitcases on his holiday. But, unlike me, Bernard didn't just **THINK** of the idea and then go back to annoying his brother. Bernard actually **ACTED** on the idea and attached some wheels to his suitcase. He started a brand-new business and kicked off a wheels-based revolution in the luggage industry.

## IT IS NO GOOD QUESTIONING THINGS IF YOU DON'T ACT ON THEM. DON'T LET KID DOUBT HOLD YOU BACK.

Imagine sitting on a wobbly chair in class. You know it wobbles. You know it is annoying. You know there is a solution. **BUT** unless you get up and change the chair, you are stuck. Wobbling.

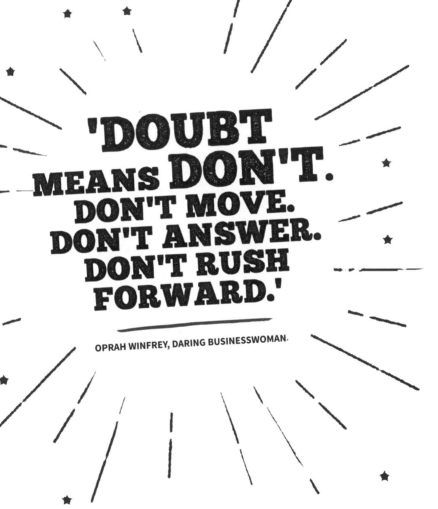

'DOUBT MEANS DON'T. DON'T MOVE. DON'T ANSWER. DON'T RUSH FORWARD.'

OPRAH WINFREY, DARING BUSINESSWOMAN.

# ACTION HEROES

Let's take a look at a few of my favourite action heroes. I don't mean Spiderman or Captain America. I mean people who have questioned the world around them **AND** acted on it. Taken control and made things better. For themselves and for other people.

# RICHARD BRANSON

Richard Branson is a super-successful businessman. Not all of his businesses have worked out, but a lot of them have done. And now he is a billionaire.

It wasn't always that way. And one of my favourite stories about taking action is from when Richard Branson was much younger and before he made all of the billions. He was 28 and had started a record company called Virgin Records, but it was early days. He was in Puerto Rico and was waiting for a plane to the British Virgin Islands when he heard that his flight had been cancelled. He was really annoyed and disappointed. He'd been away from his girlfriend for three weeks and was really desperate to see her.

So he had two choices:

## CHOICE 1
### BE AN ACTION HERO.

**1** Question whether he really is going to have to wait days for the next plane.

**2** Think of a solution.

**3** Act on it!

## CHOICE 2
### DO NOTHING.

**1** Don't question anything.

**2** Sit down in the airport café (if there is one).

**3** Wait.

**4** Wait some more.

**5** Hope the next flight doesn't get cancelled.

**6** Maybe or maybe not leave Puerto Rico. Ever.

115

**Richard Branson chose to be an action hero.**

He phoned up a company that rented out aeroplanes, asking them how much it would cost to hire a plane that would fly from Puerto Rico to the British Virgin Islands right away. Once he'd got the price, he divided it by the number of other angry people that couldn't get home either because they had been due to fly on the same cancelled plane. $39 each. That didn't seem too unreasonable. So he wrote on a blackboard that he was offering a flight back to the British Virgin Islands for $39 and showed it to everyone waiting at the airport.

You won't be surprised to hear that it wasn't long before he was in a plane back to the British Virgin Islands along with a bunch of new best friends. But perhaps you'll be more surprised to hear that **THAT** is how Richard Branson got the idea to start a brand-new airline called Virgin Atlantic.

# MELATI AND ISABEL WIJSEN

These sisters from Bali were aged just ten and twelve when they learnt about the country of Rwanda's ban on plastic bags. They began to think about whether they could do something similar in their native Bali.

They had two choices:

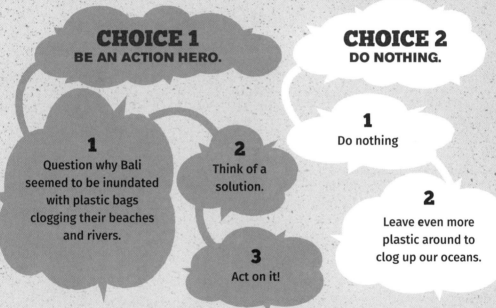

**CHOICE 1**
**BE AN ACTION HERO.**

**1**
Question why Bali seemed to be inundated with plastic bags clogging their beaches and rivers.

**2**
Think of a solution.

**3**
Act on it!

**CHOICE 2**
**DO NOTHING.**

**1**
Do nothing

**2**
Leave even more plastic around to clog up our oceans.

**The Wijsen sisters chose to be action heroes.**

They established a campaign called Bye Bye Plastic Bags, aiming to eradicate the use of plastic bags in Bali and beyond. They started by organising beach cleans, but before long they were petitioning their government to help reduce the use of plastic bags. Bali is now plastic-bag-free.

# KELVIN DOE

Kelvin was born in Freetown, the capital of Sierra Leone. The city had quite an unreliable electricity supply and so there were frequent black outs. By the time he was ten years old, he was starting to feel like this was less than ideal.

So he had two choices:

## CHOICE 1
### BE AN ACTION HERO.

**1** Question whether there was anything to be done about the electricity blackouts.

**2** Think of a solution.

**3** Act on it!

## CHOICE 2
### DO NOTHING.

**1** Wait for the next electricity blackout.

**2** Sit in the dark for ages.

**3** Hope the electricity comes back on at some point.

**4** Sit in the dark the next time it happens.

**Kelvin Doe chose to be an action hero.**

He started to collect scrap metal, discarded devices and rubbish, and then taught himself to build a battery. It powers his home and all the other homes in his neighbourhood – and Kelvin's action has inspired a generation of young people from Sierra Leone to believe that anything is possible with dedication.

# NICHOLAS LOWINGER

At a very young age, Nicholas visited a homeless shelter with his mother. He was devasted to see that some of the people there had no shoes. One brother and sister went to school on alternate days because they only had one pair of shoes between them.

Nicholas had two choices:

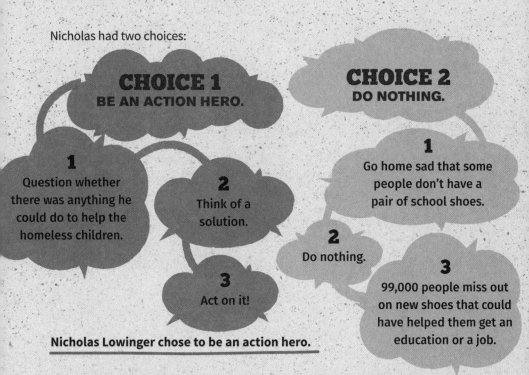

**CHOICE 1**
BE AN ACTION HERO.

**1** Question whether there was anything he could do to help the homeless children.

**2** Think of a solution.

**3** Act on it!

**CHOICE 2**
DO NOTHING.

**1** Go home sad that some people don't have a pair of school shoes.

**2** Do nothing.

**3** 99,000 people miss out on new shoes that could have helped them get an education or a job.

**Nicholas Lowinger chose to be an action hero.**

After visiting the shelter, he raced home, collected all the shoes he could and donated them to the homeless shelter. But once he got there, he realised that not everyone at the homeless shelter was the same shoe size as him. Undeterred, Nicholas started an initiative called Gotta Have Sole that supplies new, properly fitting shoes to homeless people.

Since then, Gotta Have Sole has donated more than 100,000 new pairs of shoes, helping homeless people attend schools and job interviews, and building their self-esteem.

# BE YOUR OWN ACTION HERO

Now, you don't necessarily have to change the world. You can be your **OWN** action hero. Questioning things and making things happen for **YOU**.

So, let's return to the story of my job at the bank.

The whole debacle had showed me that it was okay to question things. My dad wasn't annoyed that I didn't like the job; I had thought it through carefully and I was able to make the change and leave. It wasn't right for me.

## STEP 1: QUESTION THE CURRENT SITUATION.

I knew that I loved to write. And I loved learning things, hearing new ideas and then weaving them together for other people to read. Maybe I could be an actual writer?

## STEP 2: THINK OF A SOLUTION.

But to make things happen, I needed to get out there, get going and take initiative. Becoming a writer wasn't just going to happen to me. So I had a choice. I could sit, do nothing and hope that someone might remember the article I wrote about table tennis for the local paper two years ago, hear that I was now ready and available, and ring me up. Not that likely.

Or I could take **STEP 3**. Act and make it happen myself.

I remembered when my best friend Mark had wanted a job as a waiter to earn a little extra money after school. So he acted. He phoned every restaurant in Reading and asked to speak to the chef. Everyone said no, except one nursing home that he phoned by mistake. And they gave him a job making the evening meal for the elderly residents. I was pleased for Mark, but I really felt for those guys in the nursing home. He couldn't even make a sandwich!

I decided to take the same approach as Mark had back then. I phoned everyone I could possibly think of: every newspaper editor, every head of sport, every deputy editor. Anyone who might possibly be able to give me a break. I even spoke to the office cleaner at one newspaper – for fifteen whole minutes. He just picked up the phone and, without waiting, I went straight in to it: why he should let me have a go at a short article on karate.

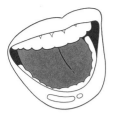

It was a bit disappointing when he explained that he was in charge of buying the bleach, but I think he felt sorry for me. He gave me the direct number of the editor.

Making those calls was nerve-wracking. It was embarrassing. No one called me back and even when I did get through, more than once I heard,

**MATTHEW FYED, YOU SAY? TABLE TENNIS? NO, NEVER HEARD OF YOU**

on the other end of the line.

But finally, on what must have been my hundredth call, I spoke to a wonderful man called David Chappell who was at that time the sports editor of *The Times*.

And he gave me a chance.

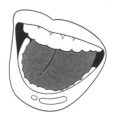

DON'T GIVE UP.
BE YOUR OWN
**ACTION HERO.**
MAKE IT HAPPEN
FOR YOU.

# OVER TO YOU

## COULD I?

When you next use the words 'I wish' or 'They need to' or 'Someone should', replace them with the words 'I could' or 'I could ask'.

Take a look at these examples:

**(1)** *'They need to set up a drama club at school, we don't have one.'*
**Instead try: 'I COULD** set up a drama club at school, we don't have one.'

**(2)** *'Someone should put wheels on a suitcase, my bag is so heavy.'*
**Instead try: 'I COULD** put wheels on a suitcase, my bag is so heavy.'

**(3)** *'I wish I had someone to help with my homework.'*
**Instead try: 'I COULD ASK** someone to help with my homework.'

All of a sudden you have changed your mindset into that of an action hero!

## GO FOR IT.

*Not everyone is kind.*

My mum is though; really kind. She'd help anyone. She'd take anyone anywhere they needed to go at any time of the day or night. She once drove me 200 miles to a table-tennis tournament and when I arrived, I rummaged in the massive, heavy blue bag (that wasn't on wheels) only to realise I had brought six pairs of dirty socks but no table-tennis bat.

**DISASTER.**

She wasn't pleased with me, but she did drive 200 miles home to get it for me. That day she drove a total of 800 miles in the car (you know, the one with **SYED BROTHERS** on the side …). I'm amazed it even managed 800 miles in total, never mind in one day.

But my mum wasn't just kind to me, she was kind to everyone. One night, nine (yes, nine) people slept in our front room after it snowed really heavily and a bus broke down outside our house. She barely knew them, but she made them all hot soup, and even gave away her favourite book to someone who admired it on the shelf.

She really is super-kind.

So, this lovely tale about my mum got me thinking…You see, she has **LOADS** of friends. Everyone likes my mum. Everyone trusts my mum. She gets invited to every party and is the first one anyone phones when they have some news to share or need help with a problem.

I remember a time when she was due to bake for our school cake sale, but she got the flu. She could barely speak, let alone get out of bed and crack open the icing sugar. So she asked my brother and me to make the cakes.

Now this was a risk – to everyone! I was dangerously inexperienced in the kitchen department and my brother had only ever baked a Christmas cake at school. His icing was so rock hard that my dad had had to use the electric carving knife to cut into it.

So we considered, well, just not doing it. We got halfway to the table-tennis centre that evening before I had second thoughts. Mum was really ill and would be so disappointed to let the school down. So we went back home, opened a recipe book, practically lost a finger each in the electric whisk (don't try this at home) and

made possibly the 12 worst cupcakes in human history.

I felt bad for anyone who bought them at school. How could they possibly have tasted good? But it was for charity, and here's the thing: everyone was so **PLEASED** with us; so pleased we'd made the effort, and so delighted that we'd just wanted to help.

I felt great for a few days afterwards. One small act of kindness and everyone was treating me like I was the best thing since Florence Nightingale (well, almost). It made me realise that

I SHOULD TRY AND DO A BIT MORE HELPFUL STUFF.

And that's when it dawned on me.

That's why everyone likes my mum so much – because she is kind, because she is helpful and because she is trustworthy. In short, she's the type of person you want to know, right?

Let's come back to this in a moment, but first we have to look at some bad news. The fact is, not everyone is kind, and certainly not everyone is kind All. Of. The. Time.

People can be unkind in all kinds of strange kinds of ways (I think I just invented the world's worst tongue-twister). They can say mean things, they can refuse to share things with you, they can exclude you or refuse to help you when you ask.

But do you know what? I think most people would **LIKE** to be kind and helpful. I bet **YOU** like to think of yourself as a pretty kind person. But I also bet that you've been unkind once or twice. I know I have – and it usually starts with **Kid Doubt** (yep, him again). When **Kid Doubt** is there making someone feel nervous, unsure or insecure, they can start doing things or saying things that they might not be proud of. Things that might be hurtful or unhelpful to someone else. That might even make that person doubt **THEMSELVES** in a horrible **Kid Doubt** chain reaction!

When was the last time someone was unkind to you? Maybe they said something that was cruel. Maybe they excluded you. Maybe you asked for help and they wouldn't. And I bet you remember it.

130

That's the thing about **UNKINDNESS.**

Its **EFFECTS** can last a really <u>LONG</u> time.

Here are some of the reasons I reckon people are unkind or unhelpful.

**REASON FOR UNKINDNESS**

They are worried that you are getting ahead of them.

They are hoping that being unkind to you will make other people think they are cool.

**WHY YOU SHOULDN'T LET IT BOTHER YOU**

Well, good for you! You're obviously working hard to achieve your goals. Don't change YOUR path. Surely they should work harder to catch up with you. Being unkind isn't going to improve their skills!

Well, this is A TOTAL WASTE OF THEIR TIME. It certainly won't actually make them successful, so don't let it bother you. Carry on with YOUR own path.

They're feeling a bit rubbish, and being unkind makes them feel good about themselves – temporarily. Perhaps because making you upset allows them a bit of control over your feelings.

If they can get in there first and be negative about you, then maybe other people will forget to be negative about them.

They just don't know what they are losing out on in life!

I think this is why people are often unkind, especially online. For a tiny moment, they get a bit of pleasure from their unkindness.

However, it doesn't last. How can it? You're not going to stay upset for ever. So they'll have to be mean to someone else. And this is a sure-fire way to end up with very few friends.

I think this happens when people are tired, stressed or a bit unhappy themselves. So being unkind allows them to forget their own feelings for a little while.

That is all them – and nothing at all to do with you! So don't let it throw you off YOUR path.

We are just about to get to this bit. And it is MEGA!

But what if it might be the case that it was just better, all round, to be kind? Well, '**OBVIOUSLY**,' I hear you shout. 'Tell us something that our teachers **DON'T** tell us fifty times a day.'

# THE SECRET OF KINDNESS

Well, I have already told you that thing about the awesome skin-shedding. I bet your teachers don't tell you about **THAT**. **NO ONE** tells you about things like that.

And what if (and this is another secret that people don't tell you) being kind and likeable could actually make you **MORE SUCCESSFUL**? What if going the extra mile to help someone turns out to mean that you are likely to have **MORE FRIENDS** and be more popular? I'm certain this is why my mum has so many friends.

You see, I really do think that most people would like to be kind. **Kid Doubt** sometimes gets in the way of that, and so they do or say unkind things that they don't really mean. But what if being authentic, daring to be you, could actually make you **MORE RESILIENT** and help you when others are being unkind? All of this would definitely wipe the smirk right off **Kid Doubt's** unkind face.

And if everyone got in on this secret then everyone might start being more kind and helpful. We might stop bullies in their tracks, we might stop online trolls in their, erm, bedrooms. This could be **HUGE**. If everyone is kind and works together, it could change humanity.

Wow, you can see where this is heading, right? Yep, straight towards that Nobel Peace Prize (I knew that clarinet practice and poetry writing was working!).

OK, back to reality.

Things are changing so quickly in the world today. Everyone is much better connected to each other, and people are working to solve complicated problems like climate change, global poverty or how robots might help us in the future. In a world like this, kindness and an ability to be helpful to other people is **EXACTLY** what we are going to need. And maybe, just maybe, there are some benefits that **WE** might reap if we are kind and helpful.

New research from scientists at the University of British Columbia in Canada has shown that being kind can help us to feel **LESS NERVOUS** and **LESS ANXIOUS** and **MORE CONFIDENT** in a social situation. They found that being kind even in teeny, tiny ways reduces anxiety.

Effectively, it helps us to silence **Kid Doubt**.

Don't worry – you don't have to donate the family car** to the nearest charity to benefit. You can start small. Can you find some way to help out at school or at home? Can you make an extra effort to include everyone in your plans? Maybe include someone outside of your usual friendship group? (And including people with different ideas can also be helpful, as we saw in Chapter 5 – win-win!). Can you say some positive things to someone who is feeling a little down?

This kindness helps us to feel more in control of our own anxieties, boosts our good brain chemicals and makes us less afraid of meeting new people. When we realise that we can actually help others, it helps us to feel good about ourselves.

° ° ° ° ° ° ° ° ° ° ° ° ° ° ° ° ° ° ° ° ° ° ° ° ° ° ° ° ° ° °

** For the record, I would have donated the family car. The one with **SYED BROTHERS** written on the side. It would have been an act of kindness that would definitely have made me feel a whole lot better too.

° ° ° ° ° ° ° ° ° ° ° ° ° ° ° ° ° ° ° ° ° ° ° ° ° ° ° ° ° ° °

# SYED BROTHERS

So what have we found out? That kindness helps us to feel better and builds our confidence. **AMAZING**. The bullies and trolls are losing out already.

But the benefits to us don't stop there …

There is lots of research that shows that being kind releases chemicals in your brain called endorphins that make you feel good. So helping your dad with the washing up might actually be as enjoyable as eating a chocolate bar. Debatable, I reckon, but the science seems to say that it might.

Choosing to be kind and not to be mean really does make you feel **GOOD**.

# DECENT DOCTORS

Three top psychologists decided to do some research on kindness. They chose 600 Belgian student doctors to do this on and they discovered some quite remarkable things. The first thing the study showed was that the doctors who had the **WORST** exam grades were those who were the **MOST** kind.

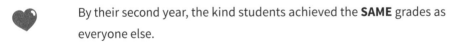

**WHAT? DID I HEAR THAT RIGHT? BUT I THOUGHT BEING KIND WAS SUPPOSED TO BE A GOOD IDEA?!**

Stick with me. The story does back me up by the time we get to the end.

In their first year of study, those medical students who helped others out, who were kind enough to share their class notes, or were willing help others with their homework, actually got **LOWER** grades.

But only in their first year.

By their second year, the kind students achieved the **SAME** grades as everyone else.

By the sixth year, they were getting **MUCH BETTER** grades.

And by the seventh year (yep, it takes ages to train to be a doctor) they were absolutely **SMASHING** it! Their grades were off-the-scale **FANTASTIC**. And their kindness was a huge factor in their success.

But why? And why didn't it work in the first year?

Well, the 'science' behind it comes down to the way in which the students were learning to be doctors. In the first year, much of what they learn is from textbooks; they have to memorise things about the way the human body works and take exams on it. There is relatively little in the way of actually treating sick patients.

Since the kinder students spent a lot of time helping their classmates, sharing with them all of their best memorisation tips and revision techniques, their classmates did better in the exams. But the exams were testing how much each student knew individually. And because the kinder students spent too much time helping everyone else be better, instead of studying themselves, you can see how their kindness might not have been that helpful for getting good grades!

But think of what doctors actually do in real life. They treat sick people. They are with people when they are feeling their worst, and they work with other doctors, nurses and families to decide what might be best for the patient. Doctors share their ideas and consider what is in the best interests of the sick person.

## CAN YOU SEE WHERE THIS IS GOING?

By the seventh year, the kinder students knew far more people. They were just better people to be around, you see. Their network was bigger, and more people trusted them because they were willing to be helpful. And so more people came to ask for their ideas. Their kindness gave them the **CONFIDENCE** to share their opinions about what treatments might work best. And because of this, they were far, **FAR** more successful in their roles.

Which skills matter if you want to be a good doctor? Knowledge is obviously important (of course, you don't want to confuse your hallux with your canthus. Not unless you want a big toe in your eye anyway!). But the ability to work with other people, to have the trust of a sick person and their family, and to have the respect of a large number of other people who will turn to you for help – that is what makes a successful doctor. Kindness is what makes that success happen.

In today's world, where our challenges are more complex than they have ever been, independent working will only take us so far. We need to work effectively with other people more and more often. We need other people to **WANT** to be in our team, to trust us, to believe that we are helpful and reliable.

The story of the decent doctors does tell us something else important too. That you can't spend **ALL** of your time giving and helping and tending to other people. Think of the first-year students who did that. They suffered by not spending enough time on their own work. It's about finding a balance, about being kind to ourselves too. And that is totally okay.

# BE KIND TO YOU!

Kindness doesn't just mean being nice to other people. It's worth remembering to take time to be kind to yourself as well as everyone around you. Taking time out to make sure that you feel okay, that you have the help **YOU** need and that stuff is not causing you to worry too much is really important.

Here are some of the things I do to try to reduce anxiety and worries:

##  FIND A ROUTINE WITH SLEEP.

My sleep routine during my table-tennis career was epic. You need good sleep if you have a big match the next day (or even if you don't, to be honest). I used to take my own comfy pillow everywhere in my blue sports bag (probably another reason why it was so heavy; if only it had been on wheels…) and I even had a black-out blanket to make my bedroom super-dark. Find routines that work for you so that you can sleep well. It might be going to bed at the same time each night. It might be having some water by your bed in case you wake up thirsty. It might be re-reading your favourite Harry Potter for twenty minutes to relax and unwind.

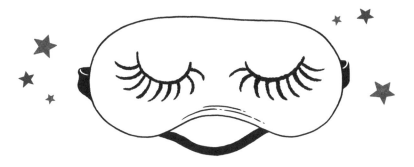

## (2) FIND TIME TO GET EXERCISE.

Exercise is brilliant. Why? Because it releases a whole load of feel-good endorphins which make you feel amazing. So ramp up your efforts in your PE lessons, take a good long walk or think about joining a local sports club. Table tennis, anyone?

## (3) FIND THINGS THAT MAKE YOU FEEL CALM.

Mine is re-watching a table-tennis match against Jan Ove Waldner where I played really well. It just makes me feel good. Obviously, yours won't be the same (although, believe me, it was a great match!), so try to find something you can do if your mind starts racing and you begin to feel overloaded. It might be reading, listening to music or absorbing yourself in a drawing. Whatever works for **YOU**.

##  TAKE TIME AWAY FROM SCREENS.

This is an important one because although our tech is fascinating, we can get consumed by it. So put down your screen and try something different. Rather than spending an afternoon scrolling or playing games online, arrange to meet your friends in person or hang out with your family. This will help you see that what is happening online is only a tiny part of a much bigger world. There is so much else going on out there – go and find it!

##  DON'T BOTTLE THINGS UP.

Find time to talk to friends, family or teachers about things that cause you anxiety. You won't be the only one – everyone has things that worry them. Sometimes, just talking to someone else is enough to banish your **Kid Doubt**.

# THERE'S NO 'I' IN 'TEAM'

Have you heard of Jonas Salk? I'm guessing probably not. But you might owe your life to him (and his team).

Polio is an infectious disease which, at its worst, can cause paralysis of muscles and even death. But don't worry, you won't catch it – you will have been vaccinated against it. Jonas Salk invented that vaccine.

But he didn't do it alone. He had a **TEAM** of people who worked with him, tirelessly testing and improving the vaccine, as well as growing the polio virus in a test tube. You see, unless you have the pesky thing on its own in a test tube (rather than in the slightly more complicated location of your body), it is hard to work out how to **SMASH** it to pieces. But, apparently, it's not easy to grow this stuff in a test tube. Fortunately, a crew of scientists had actually won the Nobel prize for discovering how to do it already (I wonder if they played the clarinet?) – and these hugely clever scientists worked with Jonas Salk on his vaccine, so he owed them a lot of thanks.

The polio vaccine was a huge success and Europe was declared 'polio free' more than fifteen years ago. But when Jonas Salk came to talk about this great achievement, he omitted to mention any of his team, or the work of the brilliant test-tube scientists. He mentioned no one – and took all of the credit for himself.

Maybe he was worried about the scientists getting ahead of him?
Maybe he wanted to be in control, to steal the limelight?
Maybe **Kid Doubt** was causing him trouble.

Whatever he was thinking, it was not a kind thing to have done. His colleagues had worked so hard, but after the awards ceremony they were left feeling devastated, upset and overlooked.

Jonas Salk never acknowledged how hard his team had worked. He never gave any credit to anyone except himself. And his team – and many other scientists – struggled to forget this. As a result, many of them didn't really want to work with Jonas Salk after that. Why would they? They would never get any recognition for their work.

# 'ALONE WE CAN DO SO LITTLE. TOGETHER WE CAN DO SO MUCH.'

**HELEN KELLER, DARING AUTHOR AND POLITICAL ACTIVIST**

The story of Jonas Salk shows us something very important about a thing called 'The Kindness Cascade'.

In the end, people who are unkind will often end up with a shrinking network of friends. People don't trust others who are unkind. People don't find it fun to hang out with or work with people who are unkind. In the end, people who are unkind are usually the biggest losers.

Kindness, on the other hand, has a **CASCADE EFFECT**. If you are nice and helpful, it makes you feel good, more confident. And, importantly, it makes other people feel good too! And then they want to help out more people.

Before you know it, you've got a network of friends to rival Facebook. Kindness really does pay.

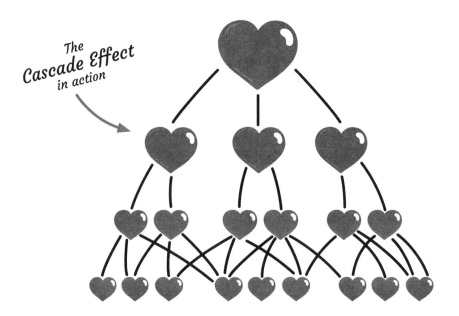

*The Cascade Effect in action*

# 'KINDNESS HEALS PEOPLE. IT'S WHAT BRINGS US TOGETHER – IT'S WHAT KEEPS US HEALTHY.'

LADY GAGA, POPSTAR AND PURVEYOR OF KINDNESS

# FAMOUSLY KIND

Need some more inspiration on how the kindness code of conduct can give you warm and fuzzy feelings?

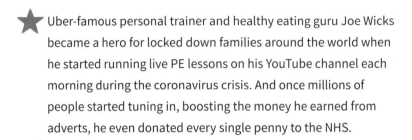

⭐ Uber-famous personal trainer and healthy eating guru Joe Wicks became a hero for locked down families around the world when he started running live PE lessons on his YouTube channel each morning during the coronavirus crisis. And once millions of people started tuning in, boosting the money he earned from adverts, he even donated every single penny to the NHS.

⭐ One of the busiest and important authors in the world **EVER**, J.K. Rowling, took a break from feverishly finishing *Harry Potter and the Goblet of Fire* to email a fan, who was diagnosed with leukaemia. The fan sadly died soon after, but she lives on as the name of a character sorted into Gryffindor – the house known for its bravery.

⭐ The 'Pay It Forward' Movement encourages everyone to do three unprompted good deeds for three different people. These deeds could be something small, like buying someone a hot drink anonymously, or giving someone on the street an umbrella when it's raining. The idea is that you ask for nothing in return, except that the person 'pay it forward' and do three good deeds for three more people. That's it. The movement has spread around the globe and even has a book and a film named after it.

# OVER TO YOU

## KINDNESS PAYS

Think about three small acts of kindness you can do for three people every day for a week.

They can be something very small like holding a door open, giving a big smile to the new person at school or offering to clean up your room or take the bins out.

At the end of the week, make a note of them so that you'll remember what they were, and how doing each small act of kindness made you feel.

# BUMPS IN THE ROAD

# 8

*The first person who will live to be **200 YEARS OLD** may have already been born, according to Professor Stuart Kim at Stanford University.*

It could be you!

And if it is you, I suspect it's unlikely that in the next (approximately) 189 years that you are going to be alive, something a little bit bad won't happen. Yes, it's unlikely that you won't have a single problem or issue to deal with over the course of the next 100,000,000 minutes. (That's about 189 years, by the way.)

This chapter is all about how we deal with that stuff. The stuff that doesn't go quite to plan. The stuff that causes us to worry. The stuff that makes us anxious. As we know, this is the stuff **Kid Doubt LOVES** – but if we are **DARING** to be ourselves and **FOLLOWING** our own path, we need to be able to tackle the bumps along the way.

There are **ALWAYS** bumps along the way…

My coach, Pete Charters, used to have a saying that he'd use if I'd lost a table-tennis match:

**MATTHEW, RESILIENCE IS WHAT WE NEED HERE. IN SPADES.**

To be honest, I wasn't ever sure why spades had anything to do with it. And what on earth did resilience even mean? Let's look at this word:

# RESILIENCE.

You might have heard it before. Your teachers or your parents might have mentioned it a couple of (million) times. But what does it really mean?

I looked it up in the Cambridge English Dictionary once, after Pete Charters said the 'spades' phrase again during a bad training session.

Resilience means:
*The ability to be happy or successful again after something difficult or bad has happened.*

All of a sudden, resilience was sounding great to me!

If it's possible to be happy or successful after something tricky happens, then maybe I wouldn't need to worry so much about losing in the first place! And if I did lose, I'd know I could still win in the future – so I wouldn't have to get so anxious about the next match.

Basically, the world wouldn't end. Or come crashing down around my ears. I would have another chance…

And, therefore, I'd be more **CONFIDENT** about following my own path if I knew that, in the end, I'd be just fine.

# RESILIENCE

It's quite an interesting word when you think about it. You can make all sorts of words with the letters in it. You can make **CELERIES**. (I really do not like celery, the idea of more than one of those evil green sticks fills me with dread.) You can also make **EILEEN** and **IRENE** – but who on earth are they?

On a more serious note, you can also make some words I really like. **SINCERE**, which is what I try to be with other people. And this next one is my personal favourite. If you rearrange all the letters in 'resilience', you can make the phrase **I RE-SILENCE**. I like that. I like it because I know that I need to silence **Kid Doubt**, over and over again, when I start to doubt myself. I need to learn to **RE-SILENCE** him each time he tries to bring me down.

Wow. Resilience is sounding like just the stuff we need in our toolkit if things don't go to plan, right? But when I was reading that dictionary entry after table-tennis practice, I didn't really know **WHAT** resilience was, let alone **WHERE** to get it. Perhaps you could order resilience online? Does it come in a box? I just had no idea. That was, until my brother nailed it …

My brother … he thinks he's hilarious. He isn't. But he does have some funny and (it turns out) quite useful ideas he gets us to think about.

153

So, for example, if you could be a cake, what cake would you be? This was the kind of important debate that happened often in our house. My brother was a chocolate muffin; I was usually a Swiss roll, but sometimes a brownie. My dad was always a rum and raisin fruit loaf (nope, me neither, but knowing my dad's eye for a bargain, they were probably on offer somewhere).

And there were others! If you could be a city, which city would you be? My brother thought he'd like to be Guadalajara because it sounded exotic and interesting. I'm not sure he knew where it was (it's in Mexico, in case you are wondering). I definitely wanted to be London. For some reason I loved the idea of having an underground tube network you could jump on to take you just 200 metres down the road if you wanted.

As I said, all the great issues of the day were discussed in the Syed household.

But then one day (and I'm getting to the point soon, I promise) my brother came up with a really interesting one.

# IF YOU COULD BE **MADE OF ANY KIND OF MATERIAL,** WHAT MATERIAL WOULD **YOU** BE MADE OF?

We discussed this for days. (Remember, TV wasn't great back in those days and iPads hadn't been invented.) Initially, we thought we'd cracked it. **GOLD**, of course! Surely that would be ideal? You'd be able to chip a bit off your left elbow and buy a house or a car, or clip your toenail and buy an ice cream. Awesome!

But, let's face it, that was flawed. Your left elbow – as with most things on your person – is quite useful, especially as a table-tennis player. And your toenails probably wouldn't grow fast enough to keep you in much more than a weekly mint choc-chip cone.

We went back to the drawing board. Then one day, when my brother was pumping up his bike tyres, it hit him…

So, and I know you can hardly bear the suspense now, what on earth *was* this wonder material?

# WELL, IT WAS … RUBBER!

I know, crazy, eh? But do you know these amazing facts about rubber?

**1** It actually grows on trees (unlike money, which doesn't, as my mum kept telling me after she had to buy a new pair of trousers for my chemistry teacher).

**2** The rubber tree, called a *Hevea brasiliensis*, is native to Brazil but is grown commercially in southeast Asia and makes about 8.5 kg of rubber (the weight of two average cats) every year – for 28 years!

**3** We make 28 million tonnes of the stuff each year, including one billion tyres (and quite a lot of table-tennis bat covers too!)

**4** Rubber is quite environmentally friendly when it's grown naturally. In fact, the USA recycles 250 million rubber tyres every year. And when they are recycled, they can produce new forms of fuel that we can use instead of coal and petrol. Rubber is win-win!

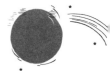

But the most interesting thing about rubber is not what we make from it…but what it can actually do!

**THIS** is what became one of my biggest strengths. Something that gave me a lot of confidence in tricky times.

**RUBBER** can

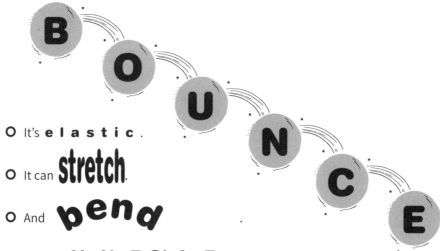

O  It's **e l a s t i c** .

O  It can **stretch**.

O  And **bend** .

O  It can **cHaNgE ShApE**.

O  It can **FLEX** to absorb shocks.
(Which is why it is so useful in tyres for handling bumps in the road!)

O  It is pretty **STRONG** and very durable.

O  It can **insulate** against heat and provide a seal against leaks.

O  It can even **REINVENT** itself when it is recycled!

**THIS STUFF IS AWESOME**. And just when we were (grudgingly) congratulating my brother for nailing that material question, something dawned on me … I finally understood what it meant to be **RESILIENT**.

Rubber is resilient.

# RESILIENCE
## IS A BIT LIKE BEING
# MADE OF
# RUBBER.

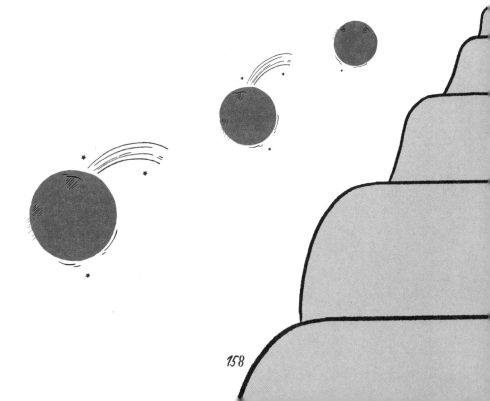

# THE GREAT RUBBER REVELATION!

This brilliantly bendy, super-stretchy substance showed me how I needed to be if I was going to deal with:

O things that went wrong
O things that didn't go to plan
O times when I failed at something
O times when I made a mistake

Just imagine if you could train yourself to behave like rubber as you go about your day. **Absorbing the smaller shocks** (just like a tyre on a car) going over the millions of **bumps in the road** that happen to us on a **daily basis**.

There is a lot going on every day. So much to think about, learn and remember. When I was at school, I could never get everything right. And if I'm honest, I used to get quite a lot wrong. I'd always be turning up for chess club only to find drama club halfway through a rehearsal of *The Sound of Music*. I was also supposed to be **IN** *The Sound of Music* (as a nun, don't ask), which made it an even bigger problem. I never had all of the right ingredients for cookery class either. I once had to make a spaghetti bolognese without the spaghetti.

**Kid Doubt** would sneer at me. Dad would flip out on a daily basis. He said my bedroom…

… LOOKED LIKE A **GOAT** HAD BEEN **LIVING** IN THERE.

I suspected that it would have been a whole lot worse if a goat had *actually* been living there, but thought it best not to question him.

And then there was that bone-crushingly embarrassing car to deal with. You know, the one with **SYED BROTHERS** on the side. Every time I got into it, I sank as low as I possibly could in my seat so that no one would know it was me. That was never going to work, was it? **THE CAR HAD MY NAME ON.**

These are the *small* bumps in the road. And they happen all of the time. Offline, online, at school, at home, with friends. It's usually nothing major, and thankfully it's usually nothing life-threatening. But it is a lot to deal with, and if you are anything like me, it might make you a bit stressed-out sometimes. So we need to get good at dealing with all of the minor hassles that occur on a daily basis. We need to be able to **ABSORB THESE SHOCKS** so that they don't affect us too much.

# BOUNCING BACK FROM BUMPS

Many of the issues you'll face will be quite small, but some might be a bit bigger. And some might even change your life. So, it would be useful to have something in our toolkit to help us deal with these tricky times – and to learn from them.

Just think, if you were made of rubber, you'd also be able to **bounce back from the bigger shocks** that happen to us **from time to time** (like a tractor landing in a pothole and fighting its way out).

**HOW** are we going to do that, I hear you ask? Good question! As I was noodling on this and wondering how that car (you know the one) would have fared on potholes and road bumps and, well, literally **ANY** bump in the road, I realised that we *already* know how to

BOUNCE BACK.

We've been looking at it all this time…

If we are not worried about being different; if we know that we can change things; if we know that we can take control and make things happen with our initiative … well, doesn't that help us quite a lot with any bumps in the road?

# YES! I REALLY THINK IT DOES!

When something doesn't go as well as it should, when you hit a bump in the road, be kind to yourself. Adjust your goals if you need to. Know that you can change things.

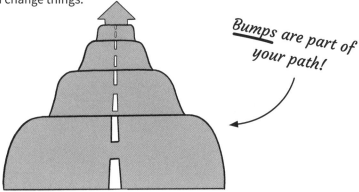

*Bumps are part of your path!*

If you need help, ask for it. Your parents, carers, teachers and friends will all be up for helping you. Especially if they are in on our new secret about kindness.

If you don't get things right first time, **DON'T PANIC**. There's always another chance. Take control and make it work out next time. The world won't end if you take a bit longer to make things happen.

# FAMOUS PATHS THAT MIGHT SURPRISE YOU

Each of these well-known people dared to follow their own path in a whole range of different ways.

# NAME: **COLDPLAY**

**ACHIEVEMENTS:** Mega-successful band that sold 100 million records!

**OWN PATH:** Right at the start of it all, a huge company called Parlophone were very keen to offer the band a record deal. Most aspiring musicians would jump at the chance, but three of the four members of Coldplay were already mid-way through their university degrees in London. Lead singer Chris Martin loved learning and wanted to finish his ancient world studies degree. Drummer Will Champion was working away on his anthropology degree and Jonny Buckland was studying astronomy and maths.

**THE TAKEAWAY:** Mega rock stardom? Well, that just had to wait. Coldplay wanted to finish their history, maths and astronomy degrees – they followed their own path. Awesome!

## NAME: **TAYLOR SWIFT**

**ACHIEVEMENTS:** Well, Taylor Swift is a pretty huge pop star, hadn't you heard?

**OWN PATH:** It wasn't always that way. The other kids at her school were mean to her growing up; they wouldn't sit with her at lunch because she was 'weird' for liking country music. All the taunting hurt Taylor's feelings, but she didn't let it stop her. She went home and wrote her songs anyway. It was what she loved doing.

**THE TAKEAWAY:** A year into her career as a massive global superstar, she went back to her home town. The kids who had bullied her showed up in Taylor Swift T-shirts and asked for her autograph. Taylor realised then that the kids didn't remember being mean to her at all – so she needed to forget about it too! She also realised that their behaviour was what motivated her to start song-writing. Her schoolmates were unkind, but she didn't let them stop her from following her own path…

# NAME: **VINCENT KOMPANY**

**ACHIEVEMENTS:** Belgian footballer who is *seriously* good at the game. He was the captain of Manchester City for eight seasons (including four in which they won the Premier League) and played 265 matches for them.

**OWN PATH:** You have to work pretty hard to be a top footballer, but Vincent wanted to study at the same time. Though it took him five years, he managed to complete an MBA (a super-high-level business degree) at Manchester Business School while leading Manchester City out each week to play in front of 50,000 fans. He thinks that some of his teammates laughed at him about his study, but it made no difference. Vincent graduated from business school in 2017.

**THE TAKEAWAY:** Even the captain of Manchester City was teased for being different. But Vincent was quick to realise that his differences are his strength. Completing his degree has meant that he has a brilliantly different skill to football. He followed his own path and had the courage to be who he wanted to be.

Oh, and now Vincent's learning Spanish…

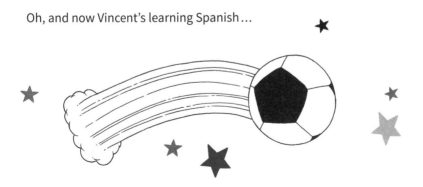

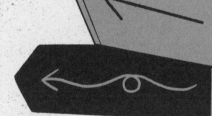

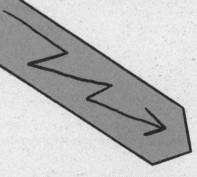

# 9

*We've talked a lot about paths.*

*And so I want to finish our journey together by telling you about **MY** path. I've told you some bits already, so you know I've had a few bumps in the road – the bakery fire was a **BIG** one – but I wanted to tell you about one of the others.*

I failed some of my GCSEs.

There. I've said it.

I haven't told many people this. It was a pretty big bump in the road.

Your parents and teachers might not like this bit of the book. They'll probably want you to pass your exams. They're almost certainly right. (Do tell them I said that, it might get me back in their good books!) But I want to show you that there are lots of different paths in life and, whatever the bumps in the road, there is always a path that will be okay. You just need to stick to your plan, take control and, most importantly, be **TRUE** to yourself.

More about that in a bit. But because we're nearing the end of the book and you'll soon be setting off on your **OWN** path, let's just re-cap on **The Plan** (AKA A Manifesto for Daring to Be You!) and my experiences with it.

# THE PLAN

**1** **Make friends with people who like you for YOU.**

Make friends with people who will build you up, not knock you down.
If you think there aren't many of those around, then you are looking
in the wrong places. I hope this book will give you the confidence to
look in different places.

**Update:**

*In the end, I gave up trying to impress Tim Preston
and Philip Beck. I made friends with Mark instead.
Apart from the shared tracksuit debacle, we got on
(and maybe this is not okay to say after the
bakery incident, but ...) like a house on fire.
He was there when I needed him, he helped
me out, and* **Kid Doubt** *was usually
nowhere to be seen.*

**2** **Make choices based on what
you feel is right. For YOU.**

There are so many choices and decisions to be made – all the time.
Make these based on what **YOU** would like for yourself, based on the

values that **YOU** feel (and know in your heart) are important. Not the ones that **Kid Doubt** is suggesting you choose…

## Update:

*I finished* The Hobbit. *I had to buy a new copy after I stupidly put the first one in the bin that day. I loved it, and although I couldn't convince the football team to read it, Mark did, and he loved it too. So much so that he even changed the name of his pet fish from Kevin Keegan to Gandalf. This isn't relevant, but the fish was a girl.*

*GANDALF*

**3** **Don't blindly copy other people. Be YOU.**

Pick out the traits in others that you **REALLY** admire and copy those. Don't feel the need to copy things that really won't help you achieve your goals or be true to yourself.

## Update:

*You'll be glad to know that I've stopped copying Kevin Keegan's aftershave and no longer ask for a Grundig radio every Christmas. His football skills were pretty helpful, but I found the confidence to believe in myself and follow my own path in lots of other ways.*

## 4 Don't be afraid to do things at YOUR own pace.

Be brave. Ask to slow down if you need to. Everyone learns in different ways.

**Update:**

*It took me 41 attempts to win a table-tennis match on the Japanese Super Circuit once. I lost 40 straight days in a row. You might think that this is taking the idea of 'going at your own pace' to a whole new level, but honestly, it took me that long to get the hang of things.*

*So take your time. Ask for extra help if you need it. You'll get there in the end.*

## 5 YOU should be prepared to be flexible.

You might not find your own path straight away, and that is fine. You might need to change it up a few times before you find what really works for you.

**Update:**

*I sometimes wonder what might have happened if I hadn't decided to be a bit flexible. I'd probably still be working in the bank. Who knows what might have happened to the bank with me there? (Though without*

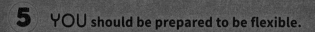

me there, it has become one of the most successful banks in the world – so make your own mind up on that one.) While I would definitely have been okay if I'd stayed at the bank, I wouldn't have followed my dream of being a writer.

## 6 Be kind. And don't listen to anyone who isn't kind towards YOU.

This one used to sound a bit sickly, but we have shown that kindness really pays off. We now know that there are major benefits to being kind – and for people who are kind.

### Update:

*I can still recall the faces of the people who bought the charity cupcakes my brother and I made to help my mum out when she was ill. (Obviously, I mean their faces before they had tasted the cupcakes, but still…) They were genuinely proud of us and remembered it for years afterwards. It made us feel good.*

**7** Make it happen. Don't wait. Get out there.
It is down to YOU.

This is **YOUR** own path. Take control. Make it the best one **YOU**
could have. Don't let **Kid Doubt** nag you about your differences.
They are what make you, **YOU**.

**Update:**

*Believe me when I say that your differences are one of your greatest
strengths. Our ever-changing world doesn't need clones, it needs
people who are prepared to think differently. So get out there. Try the
wheels on the suitcase, read* The Hobbit *if you want to, ask someone
to give you a chance...but whatever you do, don't try to share a
tracksuit with anyone.*

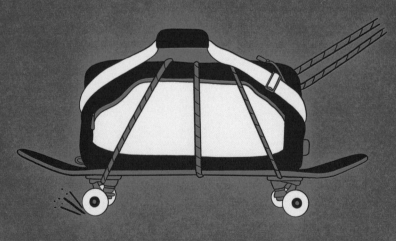

That was my **Plan**, and so far, it's worked pretty well for me. But of course, only follow my manifesto if you truly believe it will help you. Otherwise, change it. Make **YOUR** own plan. One that works for **YOU**.

So, back to those exams. The exams that I failed.

I didn't fail all of them. But I did fail some of them. Looking back now, I didn't work as hard as I could have done. Which (note to your parents and teachers) I do regret. Big time.

At the time, I was focused on table tennis and things were going really well with that. I was the national champion and I had a chance of going to the Olympics. I *really* wanted to go the Olympics.

I put all of my effort into that, and not quite as much into my algebra, my geography or my English comprehension.

Now, I could have gone to three Olympics, but I only managed two. I didn't qualify for Atlanta, **JUST** missing out in qualification when I lost to Zoltan Bátorfi. This was another big bump in the road. I was devastated – and I almost quit.

But I didn't. I carried on. I trained harder than ever to make it to the next Olympics. But in the meantime I had four years to wait, and this bump in the road had got me thinking. For the first time, I started to consider:

**WHAT IF I DID NEED TO QUIT TABLE TENNIS AT SOME TIME IN THE FUTURE? WHAT ON EARTH WOULD I DO?**

I didn't have many qualifications. I had a good forehand smash, but I wasn't all that qualified to do very much else. (Except annoy my brother, of course; I was a world expert at that.)

What was my path going to look like without table tennis? I decided to take control. I decided that it wasn't too late to finish my exams. Okay, so I'd be a few years older than everyone else taking them, but this was **MY PATH** – and I wasn't going to let **Kid Doubt**, or anyone else, put me off.

So I got the textbooks. I got the past exam papers. I sat myself in the loft of our house (it was nice and warm) and I set about teaching myself to pass my exams.

I wouldn't necessarily recommend this approach. It was really hard. The whole thing would have been much easier if I had just done it at school, with actual teachers and actual equipment and actual lessons.

Anyway, it was too late for that. There I was, every night, either in the loft with my brother's Madonna CD blaring through the floorboards, or sharing a room with Carl Prean at training camp. The rest of the team would be reading about football and Kevin Keegan, while I'd be poring over *Bostock and Chandler: Pure Mathematics 1*. I think the team laughed at me. In fact, I am pretty sure they did.

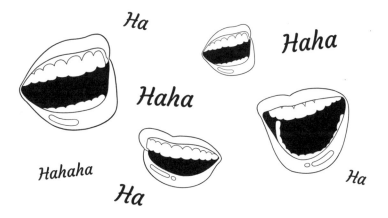

But **THIS WAS MY PATH**. I decided that I didn't care what anyone else thought. I was going to do this.

The week of the exams came around. I had to go to a special hall in London called William Goodenough House. I can remember it clearly. I loved the name. If William was, then maybe I was Goodenough too?

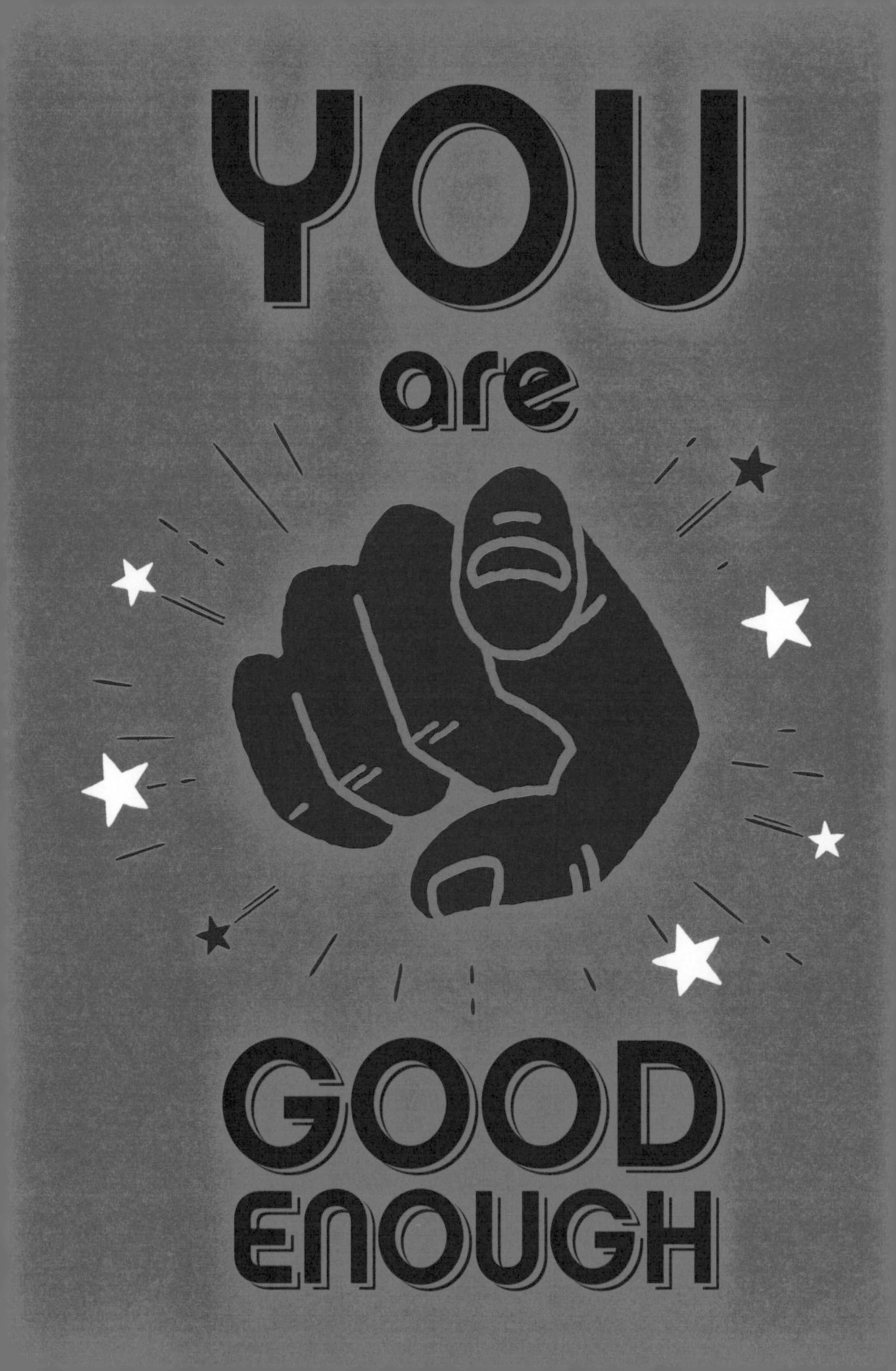
YOU
are
GOOD
ENOUGH

I was so nervous that I went the wrong way the first time I went there. My track record on the exam-passing front was not good and in my mild panic I had forgotten to take a map with me. I ended up in what appeared to be the world's largest post office. It was like some kind of bad dream: there were red vans everywhere, but no sign of anyone waiting to do a maths exam. One of the postmen (they are **VERY** good with addresses) took pity on me and walked me to William Goodenough House. An act of kindness that has stayed with me for ever.

I was almost late, but I made it.

And I passed.

All of my exams.

I went to university with the grades I got from those exams. It was a great university, and although I got there later than everyone else, it didn't matter.

I was less fashionable than everyone else too. They couldn't understand why I only ever wore a tracksuit. But I was still playing table tennis (though mainly I just liked tracksuits), and anyway,

**THIS WAS MY PATH.**

I carried on playing table tennis all the way through my studies. I managed to find the time to do both. I wanted to because **THIS WAS MY PATH**. And after I had finished my degree, I decided I would move to a town where all the best table-tennis players lived so that I had the best training partners.

However, this new town was another bump in the road for me. **Kid Doubt** was back. In fact, he was practically living right under my bed! For some reason, I couldn't seem to make friends in this new town; I just didn't quite fit in.

I wasn't sure exactly what to do until I remembered **The Plan**. My manifesto. So I decided to make a change. I moved to a different town. **THIS WAS MY PATH**.

Now that might sound a bit drastic, moving to a different town to find new friends. Not everyone can do something as major as that. But it made me realise that it's worth making even a small change if you feel that you'd like to meet some new people. Who will like you for **YOU**.

While I had to travel further to practise, it was one of the best changes I ever made. That is why I am sure that if you haven't met the right friends yet, there are plenty of other places you can look. It worked for me and it can for you. On the first night in the new place, I made friends with four people who were some of the kindest people I had ever come across. They became some of my greatest friends – and still are today.

I didn't do well at the Sydney Olympics. I lost in the first match. It was a huge bump in the road – the Olympic dream was definitely over. So I did actually quit, but luckily I was ready. I'd done my exams, and I got the job with the 'movers and shakers' at the bank. And the rest you know (unless you really have skipped to practically the last page of the book. Eye roll).

So here I am. **STILL ON MY PATH** – where people seem to like that I think a bit differently. And, fortunately, no one cares that I still love a tracksuit…

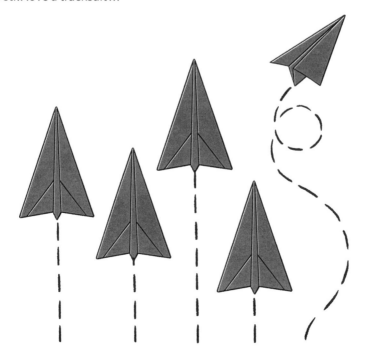

I'm still keen to try new things, to question the world around me. And I am so curious about what the future holds. There will be more bumps in the road, that's for sure. There will be more times when I will need to change things up. Who knows, a robot might write my next book and I'll have to figure out something new to do instead. But I've loved the journey so far.

*Matthew's next book*

That's because I know that (well, since the bakery fire, anyway…) I have been in control, I have made things happen for **ME**. It has been **MY OWN PATH**.

So I dare you now… let go of your **Kid Doubt**. Go for it (and I mean really **GO FOR IT**). Be your own action hero and follow **YOUR** own path.

Remember, **You Are Awesome**. So…

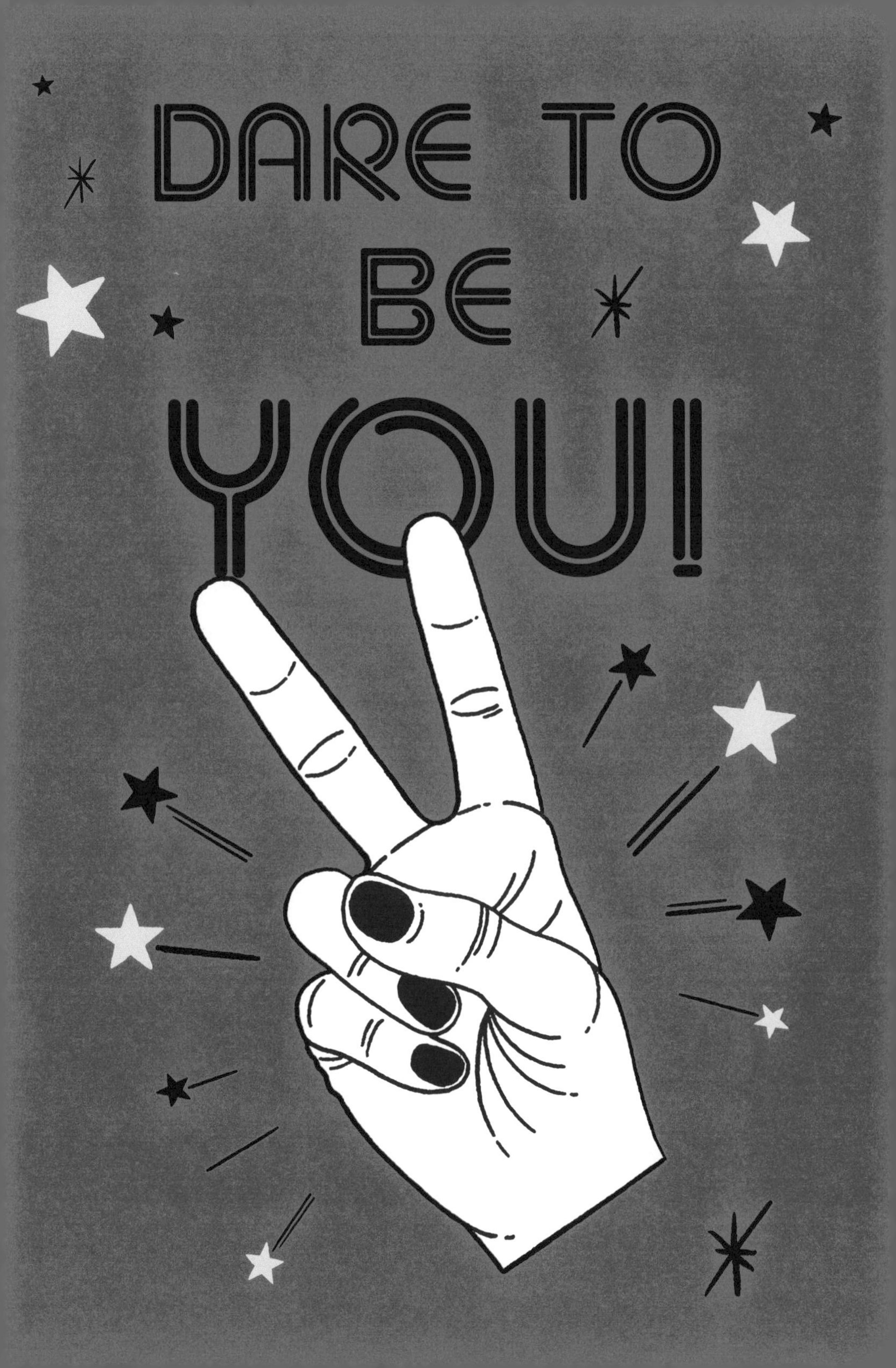
DARE TO
BE
YOU!

# INDEX

## A

act/action, on ideas 104, 106, 114–121, 124, 125, 182
actions (to fit in) 16, 19 see also copying
adaptability 55, 98, 100
ADHD 51
Alexa, Amazon 95
anxiety 10, 12, 13, 16, 22, 46, 84, 136, 141, 143, 151, 152
attitude 76, 98
authenticity 135
autism 43, 65
average 27, 28, 30, 34, 39, 41, 156

## B

balance 140
balanced diet 36
Bátorfi, Zoltan 175
behaviour, copying 24, 59, 61, 74–87
being cool 8, 12, 13, 16, 59, 61, 62–3, 84, 132, 126–149
belief (in self) 16, 91, 140, 171
Beyoncé 82, 83, 86
Bill and Melinda Gates Foundation 43
Bloom, Benjamin 43
Branson, Richard 56, 114–16
Brin, Sergey 53
Buckland, Jonny 165
bullies 135, 134, 166
brain freeze 65
breathing 66, 141
Brontë sisters 106–7

## C

calm, finding 142
cascade effect 146
Center for American Entrepreneurship 56
Champion, Will 165
change 19, 57, 58, 63, 70, 93, 98, 100, 101, 104, 105, 107, 111, 120, 132, 135, 157, 162, 163, 172, 175, 180, 182
Chappell, David 123
charity 129, 136, 173
Charters, Pete 151, 152
chess 51, 160
Chih-Yuan, Yang 54
choices 113, 115, 117, 118, 119, 120
climate change 104, 135
clones, avoiding 72–87
cockpit, size of 33–5
Coldplay 16, 165
confidence 17, 22, 24, 75, 93, 134, 140, 157, 170, 171
consequences 10, 15
control 70, 103, 105, 114, 133, 136, 144, 163, 169, 174, 176, 182
Copernicus 99
copying 73–87
coronavirus 94, 98, 148
courage 83, 85, 92, 105, 167
crafting 68, 109
curiosity 18, 88–107, 182

## D

Dance 51
Daniels, Gilbert S 34
differences, celebrating 58, 62, 64, 71, 89, 167, 174
Doe, Kevin 118
drawing 68, 142
dyslexia 43, 57

# E

electricity, invention of 100
endorphins 134, 142
evolution, human 76
exams 8, 139, 169, 175, 176, 177, 179, 181
exercise (for well-being) 142

# F

Facebook 94, 146
Filo, David 54
fitting in 102
flexibility 19, 55, 93, 100, 172
football 10, 11, 13, 74, 75, 76, 78, 82, 85, 90, 167, 171, 177
friends 8, 12, 13, 16, 18, 20, 24, 44, 51, 107, 116, 128, 133, 135, 136, 143, 146, 161, 163, 170, 180, 181

# G

glass-blowing 68
Glastonbury 83
goals/dreams 22, 84, 87, 91, 93, 132, 163, 171, 173, 181
Google 53, 94, 96
Gotta Have Sole 119
Great Rubber Revelation, The 159

# H

Harry Potter 141, 148
Henrich, Joseph 79, 80
hobbies 67, 69, 71

# I

immigrants 54–56, 70
insecurity 30

# K

Kamprad, Ingvar 56
Kauffman Foundation 54
Keegan, Kevin 74–82, 90, 171, 177
Keller, Helen 145
Kim, Professor Stuart 151
kindness 85, 129, 134, 136–7, 138–140, 141, 146, 147, 148, 149, 163, 173, 179
Kindness Cascade, The 146
Kompany, Vincent 167

# L

Lady Gaga 147
likeability 134
Lowinger, Nicholas 119

# M

magic 68
Manchester City 167
manifesto (for self) 17, 18, 90, 169, 174, 180
Martin, Chris 16, 165
medicines 44, 67, 69
Microsoft 64
military, US 33–34
money, development of 99
music, playing 67, 68, 84, 165, 166
music, streaming 31, 44, 142

# N

NASA 64
negativity, effects of 133
nervousness 16, 22, 25, 130, 136, 179
new ideas 19, 24, 52, 55, 60–65, 69, 71, 120, 136, 139, 140, 153
Nightingale, Florence 129
Nobel Prize 67, 69, 144
Nooyi, Indra 53

# O

Obama, Michelle 20
Oliver, Jamie 56
Olympics, the 13, 175, 176, 181
one size fits all approach 33, 40, 43, 47
over-copy 79, 81, 82, 83, 84, 89
over-imitate 79

# P

painting 67, 68
Pakistan 50, 70, 173
panic 7, 14, 163, 179
pathway (to confidence) 17, 19, 24, 61, 70, 93, 102, 132, 133, 151, 152, 163, 164, 166, 167, 169–183
Pay It Forward Movement 128
Pepsi 53, 82, 83, 86
perfection 22, 30, 33, 34, 40, 41, 80
performing 53, 68
Picasso, Pablo 106
Plan, The 17, 18, 19, 90, 92, 102, 169, 170–71, 180
plastic, invention of/banning 101, 117
playlist, personal 45
plays, writing 68
poetry 67, 68, 69, 135
Pokémon 94

# Q

questioning (attitude) 17, 18, 83, 93, 98, 101, 102, 103, 104, 105, 107, 109, 111, 112, 115, 117, 118, 119, 120, 182

# R

resilience 17, 151–53, 158
Rowling, J.K. 158
rubber (metaphor for resilience) 109, 155–59, 162

# S

Sadow, Bernard 112
Salk, Jonas 144–46
SAP 65
science (of success) 18, 76, 79, 137, 139
screentime 143
sculpture 67, 68
self-kindness 141
Sheeran, Ed 44, 84
sincerity 153
sleep, routine for 141
social media 84 see also Facebook, YouTube
solutions, finding 111–119, 120
strategies 17, 19, 89
strengths, finding 65, 71, 89, 157, 167, 174
success 20, 24, 52, 54, 57, 76, 79, 82, 84, 85, 106, 114, 312, 134, 139, 140, 152
Sugar, Lord 56
Swift, Taylor 44, 166

# T

table tennis 74, 86, 89, 91, 92, 109, 120, 123, 127, 141, 142, 151, 153, 156, 172, 175, 176, 179, 180
talking, for well-being 143
teamwork 63, 64, 65, 140, 144–5, 167
telephone, invention of 100
The Hobbit 10, 13, 15, 75, 171, 174
The Times 123
Thunberg, Greta 66, 104
Tolkien, J.R.R. 10
toolkit (for resilience) 153, 162
traits, positive 85, 171
trolls 135, 137

# U

uniqueness 37, 43, 58, 65, 89
universe, understanding of 99
unkindness, effects of 133

# V

Virgin Galactic 95 *see also* Branson, Richard
visual learning 43
voice; in head 12, 90

# W

Wass, Dr Sam 102
Watson, Emma 21
Wembley Stadium 20
Wham! 45
Wicks, Joe 148
Wijsen, Melati and Isabel 117
Winfrey, Oprah 113
World of Good Ideas, The 60, 62, 64, 65
worry, overcoming 12, 19, 22, 25, 43, 141, 143, 151

# Y

Yahoo! 54
Yang, Jerry 54, 55
Yousafzai, Malala 83, 103
YouTube 84, 100

# Z

Zoom 93

# REFERENCES

### CHRIS MARTIN
McLean, Craig. 'Gentlemen Players.' *The Daily Telegraph*, 2 October 2002 (spoken statement). https://www.telegraph.co.uk/culture/4729014/Gentlemen-players.html, accessed 23 March 2020.

### MICHELLE OBAMA
Obama, Michelle. *Becoming.* London: Viking, 2018.

### EMMA WATSON
Gevinson, Tavi. 'I Want It to Be Worth It: An Interview with Emma Watson.' *Rookie*, 27 May 2013 (spoken statement). https://www.rookiemag.com/2013/05/emma-watson-interview/2/, accessed 23 March 2020.

### MAYA ANGELOU
BBC. 'Maya Angelou: In her own words.' *BBC News*, 28 May 2014 (reported statement). https://www.bbc.co.uk/news/world-us-canada-27610770, accessed 23 March 2020.

### GRETA THUNBERG (I)
Thunberg, Greta (GretaThunberg). *Twitter.com*. 31 August 2019. https://twitter.com/gretathunberg/status/1167916177927991296?lang=en, accessed 23 March 2020.